SUPPORTIVE
SUPERVISION

CORWIN PRESS

The Corwin Press logo—a raven striding across an open book—represents the union of courage and learning. Corwin Press is committed to improving education for all learners by publishing books and other professional development resources for those serving the field of K–12 education. By providing practical, hands-on materials, Corwin Press continues to carry out the promise of its motto: **"Helping Educators Do Their Work Better."**

SUPPORTIVE SUPERVISION

Becoming a Teacher of Teachers

A Joint Publication

NATIONAL ASSOCIATION
OF SECONDARY SCHOOL
PRINCIPALS

CORWIN
PRESS

Albert J. Coppola ~ Diane B. Scricca ~ Gerard E. Connors

CORWIN PRESS
A Sage Publications Company
Thousand Oaks, California

For information:

Corwin Press
A Sage Publications Company
2455 Teller Road
Thousand Oaks, California 91320
www.corwinpress.com

Sage Publications Ltd.
1 Oliver's Yard
55 City Road
London EC1Y 1SP
United Kingdom

Sage Publications India Pvt. Ltd.
B-42, Panchsheel Enclave
Post Box 4109
New Delhi 110 017 India

Printed in the United States of America

Library of Congress Cataloging-in-Publication Data

Coppola, Albert J.
Supportive supervision : becoming a teacher of teachers / by Albert J. Coppola,
Diane B. Scricca, and Gerard E. Conners.
     p. cm.
Includes bibliographical references and index.
ISBN 0-7619-3188-0 (cloth) — ISBN 0-7619-3189-9 (paper)
    1. School supervision. 2. Teachers—In-service training. 3. Teachers—Rating of.
I. Scricca, Diane B. II. Conners, Gerard E. III.
Title.
LB2806.4.C66 2004
371.2'03—dc222   2003022789

04 05 06 10 9 8 7 6 5 4 3 2 1

Acquisitions Editor:	Robert D. Clouse
Editorial Assistant:	Jingle Vea
Production Editor:	Kristen Gibson
Copy Editor:	Kris Bergstad
Typesetter:	C&M Digitals (P) Ltd.
Indexer:	Dr. Kathleen E. Del Monte
Cover Designer:	Tracy E. Miller

Contents

List of Figures

Preface

TODAY'S SUPERVISOR

Like most new building-level supervisors, you have probably received little training for the job you are now asked to perform. Despite the graduate courses in supervision, administration, and curriculum development you may have taken, no one has really prepared you for the day-to-day responsibilities and realities of this job. You ask yourself: How do I deal responsibly and efficiently with the day-to-day business of supervising teachers? How do I structure my day and find the time to attend to the myriad administrative, curricular, and supervisory tasks before me? Support from colleagues in similar positions is warm and encouraging but fleeting, and although you would welcome a mentoring program, none exists at your school. You are mostly left to your own devices, learning what to do and how to do it on the job, doing the best you can as you go along. Like thousands of other men and women in building-level supervisory positions in schools all across America, you have been given a new job with few of the necessary support and training opportunities you will need to be successful. *The sad irony is that while your own training needs are overlooked, you are expected to provide ongoing professional training for your staff.*

This book is designed to give you the professional help and training you need. However, we did not write this book with only beginning administrators in mind; veteran supervisors will also find it a valuable resource. Whatever your level of experience, Supportive Supervision is a method, a process, and a guide that will help you do your job. Not only will our program help you perform your job well, it will provide you with a clear direction and focus as you develop and enhance the personal qualities and skills you will need as a building-level supervisor. Supportive Supervision takes a step-by-step process approach to all facets of instructional leadership. In this book you will find individual chapters on goal setting, instructional planning, observation, staff development, extensive professional commitment, and evaluation. By using many examples, practical illustrations, realistic situations, sample documents, and useful forms,

Supportive Supervision offers a clear, fully developed, and focused plan to follow as you supervise your teachers. In this book practitioners will find a very useful, very readable, and hands-on guidebook that will help fill the gap created by schools and districts unable to allocate sufficient resources to the staff development and training of its supervisors.

The Supportive Supervision program will do more than just fill this training gap. It will help you as a new or experienced supervisor become an outstanding leader. It is our firm belief that despite the many different and contradictory roles you are often called upon to play, that to become a truly outstanding leader, you must recognize that your first priority is to become an *instructional* leader. Now more than ever, with the passage of the No Child Left Behind legislation, we are accountable for providing quality instruction so that all children reach proficiency levels. In order to create an outstanding and creative teaching staff, in order to create a school that provides an appropriate and challenging education for all its students, it is more important than ever that we develop the personal qualities and the supervisory skills and behaviors to become true instructional leaders in a student-centered environment. As the problems associated with a growing teacher shortage become more severe—lateral entry teachers, underprepared teachers, teachers teaching out of field—the need for better instructional leadership and better supervision grows stronger. Above all else, we must all become what our educational systems need most. As supervisors, each of us must strive to become what we like to call a *teacher of teachers*.

SUPPORTIVE SUPERVISION WORKS

The Supportive Supervision program is a proven methodology that has demonstrated results in improved instruction and academic performance. The program was evolved over time by practicing administrators in the nationally recognized district of excellence, the Sewanhaka Central High School District in New York. A recipient of numerous awards, including the prestigious New York State Excelsior Award for academic achievement, the Sewanhaka district is made up of five large, comprehensive Grade 7 to 12 schools offering a wide variety of academic, technical, and vocational programs. The Supportive Supervision program gained its clearest expression in the two most successful schools in the district, New Hyde Park Memorial High School and Elmont Memorial High School. Both schools have been nationally recognized as Blue Ribbon Schools of Excellence, and *Redbook* magazine awarded each school its highest recognition for overall excellence.

Although research shows only an indirect link between leadership behaviors and student achievement,[1] creating a supportive culture of instructional leadership in the school can and does lead to academic improvement. With the Supportive Supervision program in place for the past 14 years, both Elmont and New Hyde Park have seen increased time on task, improved instructional delivery, and dramatic rises in their students' academic achievement. With a 95% minority enrollment, Elmont has maintained a 99% graduation rate for the past seven years, and an impressive 95% of its graduates go on to attend college. Over the course of the past ten years, the number of students receiving Regents diplomas (the most rigorous academic program) more than doubled, the number of AP scholars jumped tenfold, and the number of students who had multiple failures was halved. Similar to Elmont, New Hyde Park also boasts a 99% graduation rate with 96% going on to college. An impressive three quarters of its graduating class earn Regents diplomas, and results on state tests earned New Hyde Park distinction for having exceeded all five state performance standards for language arts and mathematics at both the middle and secondary levels. Finally, for the past several years both Elmont and New Hyde Park have achieved high school dropout rates well below 1%. The state performance standard is 5%.[2] Both schools are well positioned to meet and exceed the new mandates of the No Child Left Behind legislation.

BECOMING A TEACHER OF TEACHERS

In this book you will discover a program that works. Drawing upon our many years of experience in education as district and building-level supervisors, we will show you how to create a clearly focused, fully integrated, and dynamic supervisory program targeting the professional development and instructional improvement of all staff members and the increased academic performance of all students. Whether you are an experienced administrator or new administrator, our book will show you how to develop trust and form collaborative relationships with your staff, and how to improve your own leadership skills and supervisory style. Using a step-by-step approach and numerous practical examples, chapters will show you how to collaborate with staff on establishing a schoolwide goal-setting process focused on academic improvement, how to implement effective lesson planning, and how to conduct supportive and meaningful classroom observations. Other chapters will explain how to recruit and hire the right teachers, how to fashion professional development opportunities to meet the instructional needs of the staff, and how to instill a culture of extensive professional commitment. Using sample reports, the final chapter will present a three-part process and writing mode for the annual teacher evaluation. Within each chapter we also weave discussion on how the Supportive Supervision program can be applied to three categories of teachers: the beginning teacher, the experienced teacher, and the marginal teacher.

Our hope is that as you employ the principles of instructional leadership with the Supportive Supervision model we provide, you will embrace the challenges of the future, successfully meet the needs of staff and students, and become an outstanding supervisor, a true *teacher of teachers*.

Acknowledgments

We are grateful to so many individuals who have made important contributions toward the creation of this book. Without their generous support, encouragement, sound advice, and inspiration, this book would not have been possible.

Al would like to thank the English staff in the Sewanhaka district for teaching him classroom excellence and a love of craft; the English Department at Sewanhaka High School for their patience and understanding, willingness to embrace new ideas, and dedication to students; Dr. Linda Opyr—student, colleague, mentor, and friend; Dr. Kathleen E. Del Monte for her patience, insights, and unfailing support; and his family for their love and encouragement.

Diane would like to thank the staff at Elmont Memorial, who have practiced the process for more than 10 years and were involved in its refinement and have truly developed a culture of professional development that has focused on student-centered education; Aaron Maloff, a pioneer in the process of instructional supervision who brought a fresh yet determined approach to helping teachers be better at their craft; Rubin Maloff for developing the initial supervisory guideline for the observation process; Arlene Zimny who believes that no matter the position, observation can be used to bring the professional to a new level of achievement; Eileen Petruzillo for demonstrating that supportive supervision will result in improved student achievement; Dr. William Sanders for his ongoing support and guidance; Dave Bennardo, Mary Hannon, and Jessica Marotta for their sample observations and end-of-year evaluations and belief in the process; and Al Harper, Barbara Bannon, Susan Brandt, and Marion O'Connor for their assistance with the observation checklist.

Jerry would like to thank the staff at New Hyde Park Memorial and Dr. Susan Kelly and Sam Backer for their invaluable contributions to the process of Supportive Supervision.

Finally the authors would like to thank Bob Farrace at NASSP for his guidance and belief in the project, and Robert Clouse at Corwin Press whose kindness, ongoing support, and perseverance made this all possible.

Corwin Press gratefully acknowledges the contributions of the following individuals:

Jeffrey Glanz
Author, Professor
Wagner College
Department of Education
Staten Island, NY

Donald G. Wentroth
Principal
Western Oaks Middle School
Bethany, OK

Kathy Markel
Principal
Dean A. Naldrett Elementary School
New Baltimore, MI

Ginger Henry
Principal
Vickers Elementary School
Victoria, TX

Scott Hollinger
Principal
McAuliffe Elementary School
McAllen, TX

John Kappenberg
Director of Research
Sewanhaka Central High School
Floral Park, NY

Gene Geisert
Department Chair—D.A.I.L.
St. John's University
Department of Administrative & Instructional Leadership
Jamaica, NY

About the Authors

 **Albert J. Coppola** served for thirteen years as the English coordinator for the Sewanhaka Central High School District and the English Chairperson at Sewanhaka High School, a nationally recognized school of excellence. A recipient of numerous National Endowment for the Humanities fellowships and awards, he introduced technology into the English program, has written innovative curricula, created multiple staff development programs, conducted numerous teacher training workshops, and has had more than 30 years of experience as an administrator, advisor, and supervisor of teachers. He presently teaches composition and world literature at St. Petersburg College.

 **Diane B. Scricca** is presently the assistant superintendent for curriculum, instruction, and grants for the Glen Cove City School District after having served as the principal of Elmont Memorial High School for 13 years. Widely recognized for her extraordinary leadership, she has been honored by both the Supervisors and Administrators of New York State and the NASSP as the New York State Principal of the Year. She was also a NASSP National Principal of the Year finalist. Under her dynamic leadership Elmont, a school of 1,900 students with a 95% minority enrollment, a 99% graduation rate, and a 95% rate attending college, was recognized as a Blue Ribbon National School of Excellence, and was named as a Best High School in New York State by *Redbook* magazine.

 **Gerard E. Connors** has been an educator for the past 36 years. During his career he has served as the English chairperson, assistant principal, and principal of New Hyde Park Memorial High School in New York. Under his leadership, his school was recognized as a National School of Excellence and a Redbook School of Academic Excellence. The Supervisors and Administrators of New York State and the National Association of Secondary School Principals recognized him as a Principal of the Year. He presently serves as Assistant Superintendent of Personnel and Administration in the Sewanhaka district.

Dedication

*It is with deep appreciation and affection that
we dedicate this book to all of our colleagues and
mentors who inspired us to become teachers of teachers.*

Supportive Supervision

INDIVIDUALIZED GOALS
for instructional improvement &
professional development

**Continually
Communicated
Expectations
for
Professional
Performance**

END-OF-YEAR
EVALUATION
– Review of
 year's work
– Bottom line
 rating

LESSON PLANS
– Supervisory
 review
– Suggestions for
 improvement
– Teams to plan
 & share ideas

EXTENSIVE PROFESSIONAL
COMMITMENT
– Advisors, coaches
– Chaperones
– Tutors

OBSERVATION
– Diagnosis & plan
 for improvement
– Bottom-line rating

PROFESSIONAL DEVELOPMENT
– Demonstration lessons
– Peer observations
– Workshops, staff development,
 conferences, seminars, panel
 discussions (based on need)
– Degree attainment
– Teachers teaching teachers

Supportive Supervision

THE SUPPORTIVE SUPERVISION CONTINUUM

The Supportive Supervision continuum on the facing page is a recurring image and central feature of this book. It graphically depicts the six elements in the Supportive Supervision model: goal setting, lesson planning, observation, professional development, extensive professional commitment, and end-of-year evaluation. When taken together, the central circle, the six connected text boxes, and the arrows form an integrated whole—the Supportive Supervision program.

GOAL SETTING

Goal Setting is the *first* order of business in the Supportive Supervision program. It appears at the top or the first position in the continuum because it both begins and ends the process of Supportive Supervision. Working with appropriate staff members, you must establish goals at the beginning of the school year and evaluate them at the end.

Setting the Goals

Goal setting is a crucial first step in our program.[3] Similar to what is done in successful businesses, it is essential that each year you establish goals. It is important that you set personal goals for yourself, and that as a supervisor, you collaborate with your building staff to establish goals for all your individual departments or curriculum areas, chairpersons, grade leaders, and teachers. These goals should be transcribed using a standard format with supporting data including the staff members responsible for the goal's implementation.

The Goal

Although they are often used interchangeably, in the Supportive Supervision program we follow Drucker and make important distinctions between the terms *goal, objective,* and *strategy*. A *goal* is the broad, general direction in which you want to go. It is the general educational change you wish to effect. A generic example of a school goal related to raising reading achievement might be written simply as "to improve student reading achievement." Improving the reading achievement of your students is a very broad, almost global educational outcome that invites further analysis and thought if it is to be achieved.

The Data

Before you can formulate objectives or strategies to meet the goal you have set, you must look at the educational *data*. *Data* is all the necessary and important information that is associated with the goal. Educational data are usually expressed in mathematical form as statistics. These can be test scores or results on standardized or state exams, course grades, item analyses of test questions, demographic breakdowns, attendance figures, enrollment statistics, or student percentages of one sort or another. In order to identify trends in the educational data, at least three years of statistics are needed. In the reading example above we would look carefully at how our students performed on the State Reading Exam *over the past three years* to better identify what needs to be addressed. This three-year comparison of test results plus an item analysis of individual questions on the exam would produce sufficient statistical data for us to be able to develop our objectives and strategies. No Child Left Behind requires each state to maintain data on proficiency levels on all students, as well as disaggregated data for specific subgroups. Using a Management By Objective (MBO) management model developed by Peter Drucker, the Supportive Supervision program can assist you in targeting deficient areas while developing strategies to increase student achievement levels.

The Objective

It is only by the careful and methodical analysis of data associated with the goal that we begin to develop the objectives to meet it. Following the Drucker model, in the Supportive Supervision program *objectives* must be data driven and carefully focused on effecting the overall change (the goal) you want to achieve. In our program, objectives are measurable and are always expressed as quantifiable statements of intent. Again using the State Reading Exam example, suppose that after looking at the past three years of test scores, we discover that the overall trend is down eight points. An appropriate objective to meet the goal of improving student performance on the State Reading Exam might be "to improve student performance on the State Reading Exam by 10 points."

This objective is clearly focused on the overall goal (improving student performance on the exam) based upon an analysis of the data (a three-year trend of scores) and measurable (10 points).

The Strategy

It is only after the data have been analyzed and an objective formulated based upon them that we are ready to create specific actions, or *strategies*, that will affect the outcome. Strategies are specific actions or a series of actions that are designed to achieve the objective. Appropriate strategies must be measurable, time valued, and assigned to specific personnel who will be responsible for their implementation. Like objectives, strategies must also be data driven. In order to reach our 10-point improvement objective in the State Reading Exam example, we would once again look at data. This time we would examine the test results even more closely to determine areas in which our students did poorly on the test. Suppose an item analysis of the test revealed that our students showed the poorest results when asked to interpret meaning in the long nonfiction reading selections. We would then be ready to develop instructional strategies to improve that identified area of weakness. Strategies might include the writing of model instructional units on reading nonfiction text, providing professional development for staff in teaching reading strategies, developing an afterschool reading program, using more nonfiction in English classes, giving more extensive reading homework assignments in science and social studies classes, or adopting different text books.

For the English Department one appropriate strategy might be written as "all English teachers in Grades 9-11 will provide lessons on reading strategies using nonfiction text at least once a week." This is an appropriate strategy for our goal of improving student performance on the State Reading Exam because it fulfills all the necessary requirements: It is directly related to the objective (raising student achievement on the State Reading Exam); it is based upon an analysis of the data (three years of declining scores, item analysis of the test); it is measurable (reading lessons utilizing nonfiction); it is time valued (once a week); and it is assigned to specific personnel (English teachers in Grades 9-11).

In addition to the goals and objectives of the school and its various departments or grades, each instructional staff member in the school needs to develop individual goals and objectives related to the overall instructional plan but clearly focused on the instructional or professional needs of that person. These goals and objectives must be collaboratively developed and should reflect an awareness of teacher needs and concerns for professional growth and development.

LESSON PLANNING

Lesson Planning is the *second* step in the Supportive Supervision program. In the continuum, Lesson Planning appears as the next item clockwise after Goal Setting, which suggests that all lessons should follow and be closely connected to the established curricular and instructional goals for the year. As the continuum makes clear, the writing, development, and review of lesson plans are an integral part of our supervision program.

After appropriate goals, objectives, and specific strategies are developed with the close cooperation of your staff, you must now focus on lesson planning. Although lesson planning is the second component of the Supportive Supervision program and flows directly from goal setting, sound lesson planning is an ongoing process that happens all year long. It is the heart of all instruction. A good lesson plan is both the genesis and the structure, or blueprint, for what happens in the classroom. Just as no general who has any hope for victory goes into battle without a meticulously planned strategy, no teacher who has any hope for success should walk into a classroom without a well thought out lesson plan. In some ways we are more fortunate than the generals. Despite having the best military plan, generals sometimes lose the battle in the field. Armed with a good lesson plan, a teacher will almost always win in the classroom.

Essential Components of an Effective Lesson

Thanks to the important work of Madeline Hunter and many other educational researchers,[4] we know a great deal about the dynamics and structure of effective classroom instruction. There is a growing body of evidence that identifies the most effective teaching practices and instructional methodologies that work best with children. We now know quite clearly how to design an effective lesson. While there is no prescribed lesson plan to fit all types of lessons in all subjects, it is almost universally agreed upon by most researchers and practitioners that the essential components of an effective lesson are an instructional aim (best articulated as a question, problem, or point of inquiry), a "Do Now" activity related to the instructional aim, a motivational component, some direct instruction and guided practice, pivotal questions, a variety of hands-on instructional activities, a medial summary, pivotal questions, a final summary, and a homework assignment.

Supervisory Review

In using the Supportive Supervision model, you must become an instructional leader who encourages collaboration and team approaches to instructional planning.[5] As a teacher of teachers, you must be a mentor and guide who supports these cooperative instructional growth efforts. You must also regularly review all lesson plans, identify strengths, encourage risk taking, and make suggestions for improvement. As an instructional leader, you should plan on spending a significant portion of each day working with individual staff members and academic or grade level teams in planning instruction. Working with both new and experienced teachers, you must go beyond a simple check that the established curriculum is being followed. You must encourage best practice, invite reflection, and teach teachers how to design effective lessons that engage all students. For the new teacher this will often mean ensuring that all lessons contain the essential components. Experienced teachers should be encouraged to incorporate new or innovative methodologies in their teaching and to share their plans by collaborating with newer members of the department or grade. For marginal teachers, sound lesson planning will be an essential building block in the retraining process.

Keeping Current

Just as we have come to expect physicians, lawyers, and even automobile mechanics to be aware of and use the latest research and techniques in their respective fields, so too as educators we have a similar responsibility to "keep current" in our field. It is important that you establish high expectations for all your staff and ensure that all your teachers are aware of and utilize the very best, most effective methods in the classroom. As a teacher of teachers, you must, of course, know and be able to teach best practice in your field. As is the case in all professions, this can best be accomplished by the regular reading of professional journals, networking with colleagues, attending professional conferences and workshops, and taking inservice or graduate courses.

Sharing Resources

Research tells us that providing opportunities for teachers to plan together and share resources is a good way to improve classroom instruction.[6] We encourage you to use a collaborative approach to instructional planning. It is important that you develop trust among your staff members and foster positive relationships. Through your example, staff members should feel comfortable sharing ideas and teaching plans with each other. In using the Supportive Supervision model, you should encourage collegial sharing, group planning, mentoring, and peer support among all members of your teaching staff. For example, with the cooperation of one of your experienced teachers, ask that new teacher who is having difficulty in creating meaningful "Do Now" activities to observe and work with the experienced teacher on this aspect of lesson planning. Teachers of the same grade level or who are teaching the same course should be encouraged not only to share lesson materials and handouts, but also actually plan instructional activities and units together. It is important for you not only to create such an atmosphere of trust, collegial sharing, and professional development, but as an instructional leader, a teacher of teachers, you should be proactive and provide the time, resources, and opportunities for these professional interactions and relationships to occur.

OBSERVATION

The *third* component in the Supportive Supervision program is Observation. In the continuum Observation appears as the next item clockwise after Lesson Planning, which is meant to suggest that all good classroom lessons must be based on solid planning. As the continuum makes clear, observations are not isolated events but an integral part of our supervision program.

Observation is the foundation of the Supportive Supervision program because it is through this process that we truly become instructional leaders, teachers of teachers. A fully integrated, sound observation process is crucial in developing a successful program of instruction, in providing meaningful staff development, and in building a great school. A strong and comprehensive program of classroom observations is a foundation block for the construction of staff development programs. Direct observations allow you to identify curriculum or program issues, build upon teacher strengths, support effective practice, and address instructional weaknesses.

The Right Approach

As a teacher of teachers, you must approach the observation process as an integral part of the larger Supportive Supervision program. Similar to other supervisory models,[7] observing teachers in our program is not a discrete process. It is not a separate chore to be endured, but a dynamic, collaborative process in the context of the larger instructional improvement and professional development program. With its goal centered on the improvement of instruction through diagnosis and remediation, an observation must be a collaborative effort involving the sharing of ideas, experience, and expertise. To effect growth through the instructional process you must build greater levels of trust with the teacher and always encourage self-analysis and reflection. Teachers need encouragement, time, and a supportive climate in order to reflect meaningfully upon their teaching. You must be a guide helping them identify and articulate effective practices, instructional strengths, and areas of weakness. As a teacher of teachers in the Supportive Supervision model, you should seek to create a risk-free environment, a positive climate of trust and respect, where peer observations are common and a partner relationship is developed with the teacher being observed.

The Wrong Approach

For too many educators, observations are approached as a meaningless ritual, as something supervisors must do and teachers must endure. In many schools, classroom observations have little impact on instructional improvement. Not properly seen as learning vehicles for the teacher's understanding of effective practices and developing skills, too many observations are conducted in a highly charged atmosphere of fear and suspicion. Under such conditions little learning or instructional improvement can occur. From the point of view of many tenured staff in such schools, observations are a universally dreaded, yearly ordeal. For the nontenured teachers, they are often a high stakes obstacle course that must be successfully negotiated without stumbling. We must all seek to change the erroneous, negative perception many teachers have of observations as a game of "gotcha."

Pre-Observation Practices

In the Supportive Supervision program the observation process begins well before you set foot in the classroom. Prior to the date of visitation, you should thoroughly review prior observations with particular attention paid to previous recommendations to identify the specific professional needs of the teacher. You must also review the previous year's end-of-year evaluation because it will discuss instructional goals or teaching skills in need of improvement for the following year. If the observation is announced, it will be important to review the lesson plan, as well. Always stressing the importance of including all the essential elements in creating lesson plans, use this pre-observation conference time as an opportunity to "teach teachers" effective lesson planning and successful instructional methodology.

Observing the Lesson

The observation process should begin as early in the year as possible in order to give the teacher time to implement the suggestions that will be discussed in the post-observation conference. Normally, observations should be one period in length. It is helpful to arrive early and try to put the teacher at ease. Sit in a position in the room that allows you to observe both the teacher and the students. Since being observed can be a stressful experience for many teachers, you can minimize tension by smiling, listening attentively, and saying a few encouraging words at the end of the lesson. As the lesson develops, make sure you observe and take notes on the items or concerns that you identified prior to the observation. All the essential elements of effective instruction must be noted as well.

The Post-Observation Conference

The post-observation conference is a powerful opportunity to teach best practice. In using the Supportive Supervision program, you prepare a "lesson plan" beforehand and engage the teacher in a directed conversation about the lesson. You ask a series of leading questions to facilitate the teacher's self-reflection and analysis. Rather than tell the teacher your conclusions, it is more effective to use questions. This helps the teacher recognize and articulate what was good in the lesson, why it was an effective practice, and what needs to be improved. In the post-observation conference you must not only encourage self-reflection, but teach best practice, as well. It is here in the post-observation conference that your skills as an instructional leader are put to the test. It is here that you best exercise your skills as a "teacher of teachers."

The Written Report

The written report should be completed in a timely fashion and accurately reflect the discussions during the post-observation conference. In the Supportive Supervision model observations are conducted as a shared inquiry process that values openness and collaboration, and as such, you should not add anything to the written report that was not discussed in the conference. However, the contrary does not apply since there might be aspects of the lesson discussed at the conference that you choose not to include in the report. Be sure to address all the lesson elements, however, and when a teacher has demonstrated growth in relation to a previous recommendation, note this as a commendation. Indicate that the commendations and the recommendations were discussed at a post-observation conference and were mutually agreed upon. Credit the teacher for the initial identification of a commendation or recommendation.

The Seven Sections of an Observation Report

Quite common because they require little effort to complete, checklist observation formats with blank rectangular boxes for short comments are not very helpful. Good observation reports are written in an essay form and are far more detailed, personalized, and meaningful than a one-page checklist. In the Supportive Supervision model there are seven distinct sections in the written report of an observation. They are an *essential data* section that records the basic facts of the observation; an optional *pre-observation conference summary*, a short paragraph indicating that a pre-observation conference was held and what was discussed; a *lesson description*, a detailed, nonjudgmental paragraph describing what occurred in the lesson; a *post-observation conference summary*, a shorter paragraph indicating that a post-observation conference was held and what was discussed; a *commendations* section, several short paragraphs discussing all the positive aspects of the lesson; a *recommendations* section, no more than three short paragraphs identifying instructional deficiencies in the lesson with specific examples on how to improve; and a *summary*, a final paragraph rating the lesson with an action plan for the teacher to implement the recommendations.

PROFESSIONAL DEVELOPMENT

The *fourth* component in the Supportive Supervisory program is Professional Development (PD). In the continuum PD appears at the bottom of the page following Observation. Although the general outline of the year's PD program must be established when establishing goals, its positioning here suggests that PD should be based upon observed needs.

As the continuum makes clear, PD, like Goal Setting, Observation, and Lesson Planning, is not an isolated activity but an integral part of our supervision program.

Perhaps more than any other part of our program, Professional Development must be fully integrated and connected to the other components. Opportunities for PD are fully dependent not only on the district, school, staff, and departmental goals that are established early in the year, but in the case of individual teachers, these activities are conditioned by the lesson planning, teacher feedback, and direct observations that are conducted.

A Traditional View of PD

While relieving teachers of classroom duties and sending them to all-day conferences has its place in the PD program, it is often expensive, and it frequently provides little direct return in the form of improved instruction. In some districts, sending teachers out to conferences is sometimes used as a "reward" for teachers who have given faithful service. The unspoken message given here is clear: PD is a perk, a "day off'" from the real work of school. Although outside workshops can be valuable when related to school goals, they not only disrupt classroom instruction, but they overlook the wealth of talent and opportunity within. We encourage you to take a broader view of what constitutes PD to include many activities beyond attendance at outside conferences and commercial workshops.

A Proactive Approach

A much wider, more proactive approach to PD is not only less expensive, but often far more effective. In the Supportive Supervision model, PD is a fully comprehensive program that includes different levels of district, school, departmental, and individual planning and coordination. It is a carefully planned, ongoing, proactive process keyed to district, school, departmental, and individual teacher needs. In the Supportive Supervision program *only PD opportunities that support the established yearly goals and meet the individual needs of the teacher are considered.* However enticing and glitzy, conferences and workshops that are incompatible with established goals and objectives should be avoided.

Teacher feedback is an important element in developing the Supportive Supervision PD program. Teachers who attend outside conferences or training sessions should be asked to make brief presentations to their colleagues at appropriate meetings and to complete a written conference report. Reports can act as reflective vehicles for the teacher to process the new information and skills acquired at the workshop, and they can provide you with the valuable feedback you will need to evaluate the program's effectiveness and its suitability in meeting the needs of your staff. In addition to outside conferences, all district- or school-designed PD workshops or training sessions should include evaluative surveys or instruments that participants should be required to complete. This feedback is invaluable in making adjustments to the present PD program and in planning for the future.

With its single focus on supporting the established district, school, department, and teacher goals and objectives for the year, PD in the Supportive Supervision model is closely tied to academic achievement. PD goals and objectives are often set after looking at student achievement data. In addition, the effectiveness and success of PD initiatives are likewise evaluated based upon student outcomes. For example, suppose that an analysis of student test results on last year's district Science finals revealed that few students excelled. Closer examination and an item analysis of questions showed particular weakness on the experimental section of the exam. You might respond with a number of curricular and PD activities to address this weakness. The existing science lab program and training manuals might be revised; new goals and objectives might be established. Perhaps science teachers might collaborate on the creation of new science lab lessons. These teachers might also receive several hours of PD training by outside consultants on best practice in conducting science experiments, as well.

PD Is Professional Interaction

In the Supportive Supervision program, PD may include the writing and planning of lessons in small groups, observations of master teachers, faculty presentations, the assignment and mentoring of student teachers, departmental meetings, the writing of curriculum guides, collaborating on mini grant incentives, interdisciplinary projects, writing new program proposals, grade level meetings, focus group discussions, providing opportunities for teachers to reflect upon and analyze their own teaching, the reading of professional literature, video presentations, teleconferencing, technology mini lessons, and so on. In short, any time teachers interact on a professional level related to identified goals and acquire new knowledge, improve teaching skills, or learn more effective strategies to improve instruction, we are in the realm of professional development. Master teachers were not born with the knowledge of how to achieve excellence in the classroom, they learned it. In fact, great teachers are great learners, always ready to acquire new skills and eager to find new ways to grow professionally. Teaching is both an exquisite art and a complex science that requires a lifetime of study, observation, and practice to master.

EXTENSIVE PROFESSIONAL COMMITMENT

The *fifth* component in the Supportive Supervision program is Extensive Professional Commitment (EPC). In the continuum EPC appears at the bottom left of the page, following Professional Development. Although it appears in this position, EPC is not something that is time valued or sequential in nature. Developing an EPC in your staff is an ongoing process that occurs throughout the year. As the continuum makes clear, however, EPC, like each of the other components, is not an isolated concept but an integral part of our supervision program.

In order to develop an excellent staff and school, an *extensive professional commitment* is essential. Although it occupies the fifth position in the program, developing an EPC in each staff member is ongoing. It should begin when a teacher is first hired, and it needs to continue throughout that teacher's career. In the Supportive Supervision program we seek an *extensive* commitment because it goes beyond what is the norm, what is expected, what is expressly stated in the teacher's terms and conditions of employment. An *extensive professional commitment* is the observed behaviors of a teacher's dedication and commitment to the school, its shared values and culture, its philosophy of education, and its students. It is much more than being "professional" in and out of the classroom. Quite simply, it is a commitment to the belief that in a school the welfare and education of children are primary, that all decisions place the best interests of the child before any other consideration. In effect, it is a teacher's child-centered commitment to be the best teacher he or she can be and to do whatever it takes to help every child succeed.

Some Examples of EPC

It is easier to understand what EPC is by describing a few examples. A teacher who has an EPC arrives early and stays late because that is when he or she can best help kids who might need some extra attention. An EPC teacher drops by the gym before that evening's big basketball game just to say good luck; attends an evening concert of the school's band, orchestra, or chorus; or is the first to help out with a fundraiser by buying a box of decorative pencils she'll never use. Such a teacher eats lunch quickly now and then so he or she can rush back to the classroom to meet a student who had difficulty finishing the test on time, volunteers to be part of the faculty-student talent show, or agrees to be the advisor to the new alternative music and dance club because the kids asked him. The most effective teachers are those who truly believe that "no child should be left behind."

Identifying and Creating EPC Values

EPC is to a large degree a character and values issue, and as mentioned above, it is a critical element in the hiring process. It is crucial that you seek to hire teachers who have the values, character, personality, and willingness to make an extensive professional commitment to your school. You should review the kind of professional commitment you expect from new teachers with the candidate the first time you meet. It is here at the interview stage that you can best gauge the applicant's suitability by examining how he or she reacts to your expectations of professional commitment.

Although character development in adults is somewhat limited, getting an EPC from each staff member you supervise is not impossible. It is a team effort that begins with building a climate of shared values. It will require not only all your leadership qualities and human relations skills, but more important, it will require an EPC from you, as well. If you are a role model for your staff in terms of your own core values and commitment to education, you will create such values and culture in your teachers.

Five Key Components of EPC

Through careful team building, modeling, and focused discussions, you can create a staff that share core values about children, education, academic achievement, and professional excellence within the school. You must be a role model for your staff, exhibiting the values, professional behaviors, child centered philosophy, and caring attitude toward children that you expect from each teacher you supervise.

There are five key elements that are necessary in order to create an environment of EPC in your school or department:

1. *Acting as a role model for EPC behaviors.* As a supervisor you must model EPC attitudes, values, and behaviors in all the actions that you take and the decisions that you make as the administrative and instructional leader of the school. As teachers are clearly the role models for the students they teach, you, in turn, are a role model for the teachers you supervise.

2. *Using a personal appeal for professional commitment.* It is best to clearly express and seek such a commitment during the hiring of new staff, and to seek out and invite existing staff to make the same type of commitment (advise a new club, coach a team, supervise a school activity, serve on a school committee, provide extra help, etc.).

3. *A child centered philosophy.* Your actions and your decisions must reflect a philosophy of education that places the interests of children first. This often quoted concept has almost become a cliché; nevertheless, it is quite simply the bedrock cornerstone of everything you do in a school. Unless all staff believe in this philosophy and act accordingly, no school can create an environment and culture where EPC prevails.

4. *Professional dress and demeanor.* You should not only act and dress the part of an educational leader, but you must be involved in establishing what is appropriate dress for your staff. Though school rules about *student* dress may vary somewhat from school to school, depending upon the climate and socio-economic and cultural factors, establishing a professional demeanor and maintaining a dress standard for the professional staff is important. What will constitute appropriate professional dress may vary slightly from school to school, but it is important that our attire is professional, and that our dress and consequent demeanor teach children that schools, similar to houses of worship, are special places where important, life altering activities occur.

5. *Extra help.* You must encourage each staff member to provide what has come to be called "extra help" for children. You must create the opportunities and find the resources so that teachers can extend themselves professionally and reach out to students to learn. These one-on-one teaching opportunities can take place after and/or before school, during lunch periods, or during a teacher's prep, duty, or "free" time. Regardless of the subject or grade level, all teachers must be available and seek out students for this one-on-one interaction. It is a vital part of any great school.

END-OF-YEAR EVALUATION

The *sixth* and final component in the Supportive Supervisory program is End-of-Year (EOY) Evaluation. In the continuum it appears at the top left of the page in the last position before the process begins again with Goal Setting. This is meant to suggest that EOY evaluation is the final summation that takes into account all of the previous elements and points the way to new goals for the following year. As the continuum makes clear,

EOY evaluation, like the previous five components, is an integral part of our supervision program.

The purpose of the EOY evaluation is to provide an insightful, comprehensive, and goal oriented summary of the teacher's professional performance for the entire school year. For far too many supervisors, creating annual evaluations can be a difficult task. It need not be. With the Supportive Supervision program, the EOY evaluation is merely a collaborative process of review and rating. It is the final entity in the program continuum. What will be new will be reaching agreement with the teacher on assigning one of five bottom-line ratings for the year: *unsatisfactory, satisfactory, good, very good,* or *excellent.* Because the EOY evaluation is an important document, great care must be taken to ensure that what is written is both an accurate and fair account of the teacher's performance for that year.

EOY Evaluation Is a Collaborative Process

Like classroom observations, EOY evaluations are process driven. It begins with *data collection.* In this step you must thoroughly and carefully review recommendations and goal areas in last year's EOY evaluation, the individual goals that were established with the teacher at the beginning of this school year, and all formal classroom observations. You must also review the teacher's schedule, including duty assignments and extracurricular activities. In the second step in the process the teacher becomes a partner in this process by providing you with valuable *teacher input.* The teacher's performance and activities for the year are crucial in creating a balanced, fully detailed, and accurate evaluation. Ask the teacher to detail information about model instructional units, awards or honors, participation on school committees, attendance at conferences, advisorship of school activities, and so on. Invite the teacher to "celebrate" this year's classroom success stories. You may also seek input from peers as well, especially in the evaluation of new teachers. A *teacher conference* should follow next. At this conference you should review the input form with the teacher, elicit any additional information, and reach consensus based on evidence on the teacher's overall performance for the year while establishing mutually agreed upon personal goals for the upcoming year. The last step in the process is the writing of the EOY evaluation document.

Writing the EOY Evaluation

In general, the EOY evaluation should include five key elements. Each of these elements should receive at least one paragraph of comprehensive coverage. They are as follows:

1. *Introduction and factual data.* This opening paragraph should refer to years of experience, the subjects or grade level taught, and a general evaluative or descriptive statement about the teacher.

2. *Instructional strengths and weaknesses.* This section deals with the teacher's performance. Reference must be made to the year's instructional goals, formal observations, creative or innovative lessons, classroom success stories, instructional diversity, student achievement data, as well as suggestions for improved performance.

3. *Professional growth.* This section should reflect graduate study or college courses taken, inservice courses, seminars, workshops, and conferences attended, etc. In addition, this section should describe the teacher's committee work, participation in schoolwide or departmental activities, mentoring activities, as well as membership in professional organizations. If a teacher needs specific direction regarding professional development, or needs to demonstrate growth in a particular area, it should be noted here.

4. *Extracurricular activities.* This paragraph should reflect the teacher's contributions to the school's activity program. All teachers with strong EPC will submit copious data in this section. Do not neglect to include everything that these teachers do. If a teacher does not participate, state this as a fact and recommend that he or she do so. Never omit this section.

5. *Summary and rating.* The closing paragraph should provide an overall rating for the current year and point to goals for the next. In the Supportive Supervision program, this rating will have already been discussed at the EOY input conference. Similar to the bottom-line rating of formal observations, we suggest that you use a five-point rating scale for EOY evaluations: unsatisfactory, satisfactory, good, very good, and excellent. Criteria for both the observation and EOY evaluation five-point rating scales will vary from school to school, but it should be provided to the teacher in the beginning of the school year. The final statement in the EOY evaluation may contain individual or departmental goals for the following year and/or some direction as to how the teacher can move to the next level of performance.

The End and the Beginning

It is good to think of EOY evaluations as both an *end* and a *beginning*. For the teacher, it is the final supervisory document of the school year and, if done properly, it provides a starting point for professional growth for the following year. It is a collaborative document that invites the teacher and peer mentors into the process of evaluation. It values teacher input and reflection. What is written in the EOY evaluation should reinforce what has been stated and discussed during the course of the year. Teachers should never be surprised by the contents of their evaluation. If you have fully collaborated with your teachers and written them carefully adhering to the principles of the Supportive Supervision program, your staff will see EOY evaluations as comprehensive and supportive documents. They will be a fair and written confirmation of their classroom teaching, involvement in school activities, and professional growth for the year. They will also serve your teachers as a road map showing the way toward continued instructional and professional improvement.

Before we examine in more detail each of the six components in the Supportive Supervision program and provide you with some specific examples and key illustrations, it will be very helpful for you to understand some theory. In the next chapter we discuss what constitutes a great school, and the educational philosophy that informs our program and the body of research upon which it is built.

What Makes a Great School?

Here we describe some of the essential qualities that constitute a "great" school. Drawing upon Effective Schools research and instructional leadership studies, we show how the Supportive Supervision program is strongly supported by this research and can be used to improve teacher and program effectiveness.

You can feel it as soon as you walk through the doors. A great school has something special, a feeling that lingers in the hall. It seems to say, "This is a good place to be . . . stick around . . . exciting and interesting things are happening here." The feeling is almost palpable, and it invites you to stay. As you walk down the halls, people say hello with their smiles. This is not a quiet place; it pulsates with energy and laughter and excitement. The classroom doors are open, and as you pass you can hear the sounds of learning, the sounds of life.

At three o'clock in great schools, you never witness gridlock in the teacher's parking lot. Teachers arrive early and stay late. You find them before school and afterschool coaching, advising, and running here and there with troupes of kids in tow. Still others can be found in their classrooms giving extra help. Camaraderie prevails in great schools. Teachers and staff like to be with each other and enjoy each other's company. Kids are everywhere because there is so much happening. Kids feel comfortable, they feel safe, and they feel at home. At great schools student achievement levels are high, there is mutual respect between teachers and students, and the walls celebrate achievement and pride in the school and the community.

You may be asking, how does this happen? How does a school become like this one? More to the point, why isn't my school like this one? Why don't the teachers in my school behave like this? These are simple questions, but the answers are not that easy to find. There is no magic formula or secret recipe to follow in making a great school. No, the answers to the questions about creating a great school require some study and a bit of reflection.

THE ANSWER KEY

In this chapter we provide you with an analysis of what the research says about creating effective schools and the type of leadership found in the very best of them. We will review this material in some detail and then focus on what the research says, and what we believe as well, is the most important factor, or indispensable element, in building a great school—instructional leadership. We will provide an explanation of what instructional leadership is, what it is not, and how it is essential to the process of improving teaching skills and the quality of instruction. We will also show how the Supportive Supervision program is an excellent way for you to implement a strong program of instructional leadership in your school or department.

SOME ARE BETTER THAN OTHERS

Our own experience tells us that some schools are better than others. In every state, in every region, in every county in America, there are schools that are doing an extraordinary job of providing quality education and excellent learning opportunities for students. In these schools students do very well scholastically, behave appropriately, exhibit positive values, show respect for themselves and others, and seem to participate in an endless variety of extracurricular activities. They consistently score much higher on standardized tests when you compare them to similar schools. By whatever criterion you choose to measure, by whatever educational outcome you examine, some schools simply outperform others. There are schools in our nation where no child is left behind! Given the same set of socioeconomic indicators, financial resources, and student composition, why does School A succeed and School B fail? This question has intrigued educational researchers and reformers for many years. Even before the mid-1980s when the modern education reform movement began to gather momentum (*A Nation At Risk*[8] was published in 1983), research connected with the Effective Schools program gave us some of the answers to this question.

EFFECTIVE SCHOOLS

Perhaps more clearly than any other reform movement in education today, this national program has identified several indicators of what they call "effective" schools. According to the Effective Schools model, an "effective" school has an orderly, purposeful, and businesslike atmosphere; has high expectations that all students can attain mastery of the essential school skills; and has supervisors and administrators who are instructional leaders. Effective schools follow a clearly focused and fully embraced educational mission, measure academic progress using the results to improve performance, and form partnerships with parents.[9] The Effective Schools program has been used throughout the United States, at all levels of schooling, and serves as the basis for several federal, state, and regional reform efforts.

Characteristics Found in Effective Schools

In looking at scores of schools around the country at the elementary, middle school, and high school levels, Effective Schools research teams have identified what they believe are eleven characteristics found in effective schools:

- *A positive school climate.* There is a positive relationship among staff members, who all support the school's mission. Teacher isolation and student alienation are minimized, staff exhibit caring relationships, and the physical environment supports learning.
- *A planning process.* Goal setting and planning are apparent. Frequent communication on school programs, projects, and activities prevails. Committees are used to develop plans and activities. Needs are assessed in determining priorities.
- *Academic goals.* Goals are based upon assessment needs and are clearly defined and are displayed. There are high expectations for both student and staff achievement.
- *Clearly defined curricula.* Instructional goals and objectives are prioritized and developed within all subject areas.
- *Monitoring of student progress.* All assessment data are analyzed and used to improve instructional programs and methodology.
- *Teacher/staff effectiveness.* Improving teaching effectiveness is a priority, and sufficient resources have been allocated to support effectiveness programs. Staff development is ongoing and based upon needs assessment.

- *Administrative leadership.* School leaders recognize learning as the primary function of school, understand and apply teaching and learning principles, and "protect" learning time from disruption.
- *Parent and community involvement.* Parent and community involvement is encouraged. Parents are provided with information and techniques for helping students learn, and there is frequent communication between staff and parents.
- *Opportunities for student responsibility and participation.* Good communication exists among students, staff, and administration. Meaningful student activities and extracurricular activities are open to all students.
- *Rewards and incentives.* Incentives and rewards are used to encourage excellence in both students and staff.
- *Order, safety, and discipline.* There is a written code for school discipline and classroom behavior that is prominently displayed and explained to all students.

Eleven Characteristics of Effective Schools	
A positive school climate	A planning process
Academic goals	Clearly defined curricula
Monitoring of student progress	Teacher/staff effectiveness
Administrative leadership	Parent & community involvement
Opportunities for student responsibility and participation	
Rewards & incentives	Order, safety, and discipline

One can hardly take issue with the philosophy of the Effective Schools program nor challenge the validity of any of the eleven characteristics it has found in the schools it describes as "effective." The Effective Schools program does not rank or prioritize these eleven characteristics because it is clear that they are so interrelated and dependent upon each other. For example, one can hardly have a positive school climate without a safe environment for children, one with order and discipline. Similarly, academic goals would not be met and instructional improvement could hardly occur without ongoing staff development and curriculum development.

Effective Schools and Supportive Supervision

Effective Schools is an educational reform program[10] that demands that administrators be instructionally focused and possess the tools to build a sound pedagogical staff. You cannot have an Effective School without a well-trained cadre of carefully selected teachers and staff. Supportive Supervision is a methodology you can use to build that cadre and create an Effective Schools environment in your school. Similar to the Effective Schools model, Supportive Supervision places maximum emphasis on developing a strong instructional leadership program. In fact, the Supportive Supervision program provides a way to implement the instructional aspects of the Effective Schools program. As we have seen, Effective Schools calls for a planning process, academic goals, clearly defined curricula, monitoring of student progress, teacher/staff effectiveness, and administrative leadership. Each of these essential characteristics can be achieved by implementing Supportive Supervision practices. For example, by following the step-by-step *goal setting* methodology we set forth in the Supportive Supervision program, you will have an effective way to put in place the academic planning processes and goal strategies called for in the Effective Schools program. In the final analysis, using the six components of our Supportive Supervision program—goal setting, lesson planning, observation, professional development, extended professional commitment, and annual evaluation—you not only can create the instructional and academic *environment* for implementing a successful Effective Schools program, you will have the tools to do so.

NASSP RESEARCH

Research on instructional leadership conducted by the National Association of Secondary School Principals (NASSP) provides an interesting corollary to the Effective Schools program. Their research not only strongly confirms key features in the Effective Schools program, but more important, it supports the primacy of instructional leadership, the very heart of our Supportive Supervision program. One large research study[11] examined 74 highly successful secondary schools to determine how the administrative leadership operates. They concluded that the *most successful* schools had

- *A positive school climate.* This is most influenced by an effective principal and a strong administrative team.
- *A functioning administrative team.* The administrative team developed problem-solving, planning, and decision-making processes with appropriate delegation of responsibility and authority.
- *Strong and creative principals.* Enlightened leadership was fundamental to the school's success.
- *Instructional leadership.* Instructional leadership was not an attitude but a process of planned change in the instructional program to improve curriculum, teaching skills, and methodologies.

Although the NASSP study's research question was more narrowly focused on the functioning of administrative teams than the broad body of Effective Schools research, it is interesting to see that the conclusions drawn in this NASSP study confirm the Effective Schools approach to school management. For example, NASSP found that a positive school climate, an important element in the Effective Schools program having influence on all aspects of a school's operation including expectations for both staff and student success, exists in all highly successful schools.

More than the Effective Schools research, however, the NASSP researchers were interested in examining how instructional leadership operates in the most successful schools. Not surprisingly, they found that there was no simple formula for success and that instructional leadership takes on many different forms depending upon the circumstances of the school. Despite the form it took and the varied circumstances under which it operated, they found that instructional leadership is the most important function in a school. It is safe to say that without a strong program of instructional leadership, no school or department within a school can be "great."

Definition of Instructional Leadership

Another NASSP study[12] interviewed school leaders at eight sites to determine how the administrative team understood and provided instructional leadership. Their conclusions are quite revealing. They found that instructional leadership was not simply an attitude nor

> . . . a discrete set of behaviors or activities such as ordering curriculum materials, monitoring and evaluating teachers, or even providing staff development. Any or all of these behaviors may be directly related to instructional leadership, but, in isolation, the specific behaviors are not synonymous with the role. (Avila, 1990, pp. 52-56)

A significant concept here is contained in the word *isolation*. What they found is that in the very best schools the familiar elements of the instructional leadership program (observations, evaluations, staff development, etc.) were not *isolated* events, but, as with our Supportive Supervision program, they were part of a planned program. In fact, the study goes on to define instructional leadership as "the initiation and implementation of *planned changes* in the school's instructional program." Furthermore, they indicate that these planned changes are manifested through the influence and direction of various contingencies in the school (principal, assistant principals, department chairpersons, curriculum specialists, district coordinators, etc.).

Characteristics of Instructional Leadership and Leaders

This research study goes on to describe in more detail several characteristics of instructional leadership. It found that instructional leadership was not the sole responsibility of the principal, but a shared responsibility. Assistant principals and particularly department chairpersons were identified as major sources of instructional leadership. They also discovered that instructional leadership was situational depending upon the needs of the school—supportive in most where academic success remained high, more directive in others where academic achievement had bottomed out. They also discovered that good instructional leadership was planned. They found that where no planning existed, no positive changes had occurred. Finally, The NASSP researchers found that instructional leadership was enhanced by common purpose (child-centered), involved risk taking (a willingness to try new instructional programs or ideas despite the difficulties), and was characterized by informed behaviors (a proactive approach to observation).

Successful instructional leaders had firmly established beliefs about teaching and instruction and worked very hard to stay abreast of issues and knowledge affecting their students and school. Instructional leaders did not ignore problems; they relentlessly sought them out. Finally, instructional leaders paid attention to the details and always made decisions in the best interests of their primary clients—the students.

INSTRUCTIONAL LEADERSHIP IS THE KEY

Although it found 11 characteristics, the key factor in the Effective Schools program and the one without which all the others could not exist is a *program* of instructional leadership. As we have seen, this is supported by the NASSP research on the most successful schools. Instructional leadership is the key. We believe it is an indispensable component of success in any school or any department or grade within a school. Supportive Supervision, with its emphasis on a fully integrated, planned program of instructional leadership, is your key to building the "great" school, the great department or grade, a school that meets the challenges of the NCLB (No Child Left Behind) legislation. We believe it is the clearly focused, dynamic integration of all the supervisory elements in Supportive Supervision that sets our program apart from others. The cyclical, recursive nature of the program, along with a primary emphasis on proactive instructional leadership, makes Supportive Supervision unique. The Supportive Supervision continuum can create a truly effective school where all students meet high standards and attain proficiency on state assessments. With Supportive Supervision you can create a "great" school.

It is important that instructional leadership becomes the primary focus of all supervisors and administrators in the school. It is the principal, department chairpersons and assistant principals, teacher mentors, peer coaches, and district-level supervisors collaborating as an administrative team supporting the teachers who will create a high achieving educational environment, and a great school. It is you and your colleagues in various supervisory roles working as instructional leaders in collaboration with your teachers who will create the kind of school in which children thrive. A school or department without a systematic program of instructional leadership may be "effective," but certainly no school without a clearly focused program of instructional leadership can be a "great" school, a place of learning and growth for all students, a place of educational excellence, a place where all students attain proficiency as delineated by your state's NCLB plan.

SUPPORTIVE SUPERVISION IS INSTRUCTIONAL LEADERSHIP

Supportive Supervision is such a program. It is a comprehensive, organized, clearly focused program that will provide you with outstanding instructional tools to lead your staff. The NASSP research and Effective Schools discuss the necessity of establishing instructional leadership in the school, but nowhere in the program or the research do they describe how to become an instructional leader. Our program addresses this. In subsequent chapters, as you implement each of the six components of Supportive Supervision, you will have put in place a sound instructional leadership program. By using our program of goal setting, lesson planning, observation, professional development, extended professional commitment, and annual evaluation, you will establish a clearly crafted supervisory plan that fosters pedagogical growth. As a principal, assistant principal, department chairperson, curriculum coordinator, teacher mentor, or supervisor you can become an outstanding instructional leader, a true "teacher of teachers."

With a strong program of instructional leadership in place, great schools emerge. Therefore, we would like to continue our discussion in subsequent chapters on the ways this one factor that can turn an "effective" school into a "great" school. In great schools, instructional leadership begins before goals are set, plans are written, and the teacher walks into the classroom. Instructional leadership really begins with the hiring of the right teachers.

Hiring the
Right Teachers

Although it lies just outside the Supportive Supervision continuum, our program really begins with the hiring process. Supportive Supervision methodology establishes the initial selection of candidates, the composition and focus of the interview committee, and the types of questions asked during the interview. In this chapter we describe a step-by-step approach you can follow in identifying and hiring the "right" teachers.

THE CHALLENGE

Who can deny that we want the very best teachers to work in our schools? Our students and our community deserve no less than the very best, the most dedicated, the most talented men and woman to teach our children. We all want the best people to teach our kids. On that we can all agree. For many schools, however, *finding* them can be a very difficult task.

Schools in more affluent communities develop comprehensive systems for selecting new staff members. For certain positions there is an overabundance of applicants from which to choose. It is not uncommon to find 200 applications for each available teaching job. Schools in poorer communities and especially those in the inner cities face a far different problem. They often find that they have few applicants for teaching jobs. Sometimes there are none. Furthermore, in all schools, finding good math, science, and foreign language teachers is a major difficulty. This has always been a serious challenge for secondary schools. Although there may be other factors involved, there are alternative and more lucrative employment opportunities outside of education for graduates with degrees in foreign language, math, and science. The problem is so severe that it has led to a national commission to study and find ways of recruiting and retaining good math and science teachers.[13]

TEACHER SHORTAGES

Recently, the problems associated with a national teacher shortage, particularly in the subject areas of mathematics, science, foreign language, ESL, and special education, have become acute. Current studies indicate that there is now and will continue to be a growing teacher shortage. In the next 10 years America will need to hire two million teachers to meet rising enrollments and replace an aging teaching force. Half of our nation's teachers will retire during this time period. At the same time student enrollment will continue to grow to record highs. By 2006, America will educate almost three million more children than today—more than 54 million youngsters.[14]

OUR MOST VALUABLE RESOURCE

Two decades of little or no hiring of new staff for the next school year are clearly over. Rising enrollments of school-age children, massive retirements, and the movement for smaller class size have placed a renewed focus on the importance of finding and assembling a strong instructional staff. Without a doubt, the instructional staff of your school is your most valuable resource. Hiring is not an exact science. Finding suitable candidates, and agreeing upon whom to hire once they are found, is one of the most formidable and demanding tasks that you face as an administrator. The choices that you make here will affect the education of the children in your school more profoundly and more lastingly than any textbook you can buy. Whom you hire to work in that classroom is in many ways far more important than what curriculum materials you use, what standardized test you administer, or what new program of instruction you institute in your school.

WHO ARE THE RIGHT TEACHERS?

The NCLB legislation demands that all teachers be "highly qualified." What that entails varies from state to state; however, it is essential to find teachers who have not only passed university and state teaching examinations but possess the interpersonal skills needed. You know that it is crucial to find the very best teachers for your school or department. But who are the very best teachers for your school? That will, of course, depend upon many factors, chief among which are the educational background, knowledge of subject, special abilities, prior teaching experience, communication skills, and personal qualities of the candidates. Beyond these general qualifications, there are often other factors relative to the particular circumstances and needs of your building or department that are important items to consider. For example, the social studies department in one high school might need both a new social studies teacher and a new newspaper advisor, or in another middle school there might be a need for a new science teacher with an oceanography background to teach a marine biology elective to gifted students. While in another elementary school there might be a need for a new drama director for the sixth grade. However important these co-curricular or even extracurricular concerns appear to be, there needs to be a careful balance between placing too much emphasis on them and not enough on what we call the "right" stuff in selecting new staff. In fact, the right stuff should fill those needs, as well.

THE RIGHT STUFF

A strong academic background and a firm grasp of subject matter should be essential qualifications for all candidates. Yet more important than these qualifications and curricular considerations is the "right" stuff. In many ways it is more important than specialized content knowledge, academic background, or particular skills. It is even more important than prior teaching experience. Teachers with the "right" stuff are teachers who have the *character, desire, attitude, personal qualities, and potential to become great teachers.*

The "right" teachers have a glowing enthusiasm and a burning desire to teach. These are the teachers who have caring attitudes, who will make a real difference in the lives of children. They are the teachers who will want to excel at their craft, learning new skills and improving upon their teaching methodology. They will work hard at being the best they can be so they reach all children. These are the teachers who place the academic, social, and developmental needs of children first. These are the teachers who will make the great school possible. These are the teachers you should seek to hire, teachers with the "right" stuff.[15]

Knowing that you can teach teachers how to teach, but not how to love and care

> Teachers with the "right" stuff are teachers who have the character, desire, attitude, personal qualities, and potential to become great teachers.

for children, research shows that the most effective teachers are those who possess qualities of warmth, friendliness, enthusiasm, caring, and a dynamic thirst for learning. When you hire a teacher to work with children in your school, who that person is matters very much. In short, in hiring new staff you should look for *character* before content.

THE TEN-STEP PROGRAM

The Ten Steps in Hiring the "Right" Teachers
1. *Setting goals and identifying needs*
2. *Recruiting teachers*
3. *Establishing interview criteria*
4. *Reading résumés*
5. *Forming and training screening committees*
6. *Interviewing candidates*
7. *Using rating scales*
8. *Observing demonstration lessons*
9. *Making a decision*
10. *Providing a pre-employment training program*

The hiring process should begin as early as possible, as soon as staffing needs are known and budgetary considerations are established. In the Supportive Supervision program there are *ten steps* in identifying and hiring the very best teachers, teachers with the "right stuff," for your department or school. You must recognize that hiring staff is not an exact science. It can never be—people are too extraordinarily complex to be fully understood or comprehended over a short period of time. We can be fooled by an engaging personality, a warm smile, or a modest sincerity that turns out over time to be anything but engaging, warm, or sincere. By following the Supportive Supervision process you can identify strengths and characteristics and hire the right teachers for your school.

Step 1: Setting Goals and Identifying Needs

The first step in the Supportive Supervision hiring process is *setting goals and identifying needs*. As noted earlier, you should begin to think about hiring new staff as early as possible. As your staffing needs for the following year become apparent during the early stages of the scheduling process, you should waste no time in planning for next year. You should plan to meet with your administrative team, department heads, and teachers to discuss the kinds of teachers that will be needed for each open position. At this initial stage you should discuss the special skills, talents, and qualifications that will be required of that new hire before you interview any candidates by reviewing school and state test results, scheduling needs, and level of teacher experience. In this way you will more likely hire the right person, one who will best match the needs of the job. For example, you should discuss what special skills you will be looking for in that new fourth grade teacher or that new science specialist for your elementary school. What particular talents should that new middle school language arts teacher have, or what level of expertise does that new high school business teacher need? The answers to these questions will vary depending upon the type of program offered, the school, item analyses of assessments, students' strengths and weaknesses, and the level of expertise of existing staff.

After specific staffing needs have been established and the hiring goals discussed with your staff, you should create a document detailing the specific needs, talents, and characteristics of the teachers you will seek to fill each open vacancy. Additional space on this document can be drawn up for special considerations (lacrosse coach, drama club experience, bilingual background, etc.), yet these special considerations should be addressed only as secondary needs, and never become the sole basis upon which someone is hired. In the Supportive Supervision process the primary consideration in hiring new staff should always be the candidate's ability to teach and inspire children.

Step 2: Recruiting Teachers

Recruiting teachers is the second step in the Supportive Supervision hiring process. No other step in the process will vary as much as this one, depending upon the circumstances of the open position, the school, the school district, and even the state. The shortage of good teachers is so great in many regions of the country that many state legislatures are in the process of adopting all manner of signing "bonuses," college tuition rebates, affordable housing, and other financial incentives in order to attract and retain teachers.[16] Some have gone as far as modifying their retirement plans to permit retired teachers to return to full-time teaching without losing benefits. For several years now, many states have opened the schoolhouse door to those without degrees in education to pursue alternative certification programs. This will no longer be an option under NCLB legislation. The need is felt most strongly in the large urban districts and the critical subject areas of science, math, ESL, and foreign language.

Yet in many affluent districts and in some regions of the country, school districts do not have to recruit teachers to work in their schools. A simple advertisement in the local press will result in a flood of résumés. For most school districts, however, getting good teachers to apply for jobs is a far more difficult task. In economically depressed sections of our great cities, getting and keeping good teachers is perhaps the most difficult problem schools face.

Some Recruiting Strategies

In addition to using recommendations from staff, subscribing to electronic databases, participating in regional job fairs, and hosting welcome day visits for prospective teachers, establishing a liaison and developing a close working relationship with nearby colleges and universities is a most effective method of recruiting potential teachers. Teaching a graduate course in school administration at a local college can be a valuable source for finding experienced teachers and/or beginning supervisors. In addition to the obvious staff development benefits, actively seeking student teachers, providing mini programs for student observers, using college staff as resources for inservice programs, and showcasing your school as a positive learning environment are excellent recruitment tools, as well.

Step 3: Establishing Interview Criteria

Establishing interview criteria is the third step in the Supportive Supervision hiring process. Before you look at a single piece of paper from a prospective teacher, it is important that you establish interview criteria. After reviewing the goals and specific needs that you have identified for each open position on the document you created in Step 1, you must ask yourself what will be the measure or standard you will use in deciding who gets an invitation for an interview and who does not? What role, if any, will courtesy interviews play in your hiring process? What will be the order of priority? How many teachers do you want to see for each job opening? What role will those special considerations play at this stage? How strongly are you seeking to create a more heterogeneous and more diverse teaching staff by giving special consideration to gender, ethnicity, and age? What are the community expectations for your hiring of new staff?

After considering all of these and perhaps other questions, it is helpful to prioritize these factors and make choices for whom to interview based upon them. It will all depend, of course, upon the number of candidates who apply. As we have mentioned above, whether you will have a sufficient number of teachers to choose from who match the profile you are looking for will depend upon many factors (salary, reputation, size of school, etc.); however, the most significant factor impacting the number and variety of applicants will be the subject matter of the open position. Like all employment markets, the job market for a teacher is subject to the forces of a supply and demand economy. Where the demand is strongest (math, foreign language, and science) the supply is weak and your choices will be correspondingly limited. Where the demand is weakest (English, social studies, elementary), the supply is greatest and your choices are much greater.

Using an 8 to 1 Ratio

In those subject areas where the supply is weakest, you would of course, interview all candidates. In all likelihood, to fill some positions you will have to *actively recruit* new teachers as suggested above. Where the supply is strongest you should likewise interview all candidates who meet the interview criteria; however, this often becomes impractical because of the overwhelming numbers of candidates who meet the criteria. In these circumstances, we recommend that you use an *8 to 1* ratio of candidates to open position as a minimum until you find the right candidate. An *8 to 1* minimum ratio will give you a large enough pool of candidates from which to select the one person best suited for the job. If no suitable person is found among the original eight candidates, an additional eight candidates can be scheduled for a new round of interviews. For example, if you have two positions open for a job teaching second grade, you should plan to interview about 16 candidates. If, after interviewing all 16 candidates, you find only one suitable teacher, using the *8 to 1* ratio, you can interview a new set of eight candidates.

This interview ratio is not an absolute limit but an effective target range that can be adjusted, as circumstances will vary. These interviews are *in addition* to any courtesy interviews that you must schedule. Once you have established criteria for the interviews and have fixed a tentative target number of candidates to be interviewed, you are ready to read résumés.

Step 4: Reading Résumés

The fourth step in the Supportive Supervision hiring process, *reading résumés*, is an extremely important function in the hiring process. For some teaching positions it is not uncommon to have several hundred applicants. It can be an overwhelming task to find the "right" teacher for the job. You may wish to do the initial sifting process, or this can be delegated to the hiring committee or its chairperson. What should you look for in a résumé? Fancy graphics and splashes of color may distract your focus, but you should concentrate on finding those candidates who meet the interview criteria that you have already established. A specific example will make this clearer.

An Example

Suppose you are a high school principal looking to fill two positions in your English department. Mr. Young, an award winning drama coach is retiring, and another veteran teacher, Ms. Blaine, is moving with her family to another state. Ms. Blaine was very knowledgeable about computers and was often a catalyst in the department for others to integrate technology into their teaching. In addition to their particular expertise, both were excellent classroom teachers as evidenced by the high levels of student achievement on state assessments. To reduce the impact the loss of Young and Blaine will have on the students in your English program, you would seek to hire two new teachers who have comparable backgrounds and skills. You have now identified your needs. Candidates with a strong background in drama and those with an understanding of and willingness to share technology and computer skills then become your interview criteria. With these criteria firmly in mind you are now ready to attack those stacks of résumés.

Reading résumés becomes a much quicker, much easier task when you have preestablished your specific interview criteria. These criteria act as filtering agents allowing you to sift more quickly through the pile to catch just those potential candidates that fit the teacher profile you need. With specific criteria in mind you can put into a secondary packet those résumés that do not fully meet the interview criteria. Applying your interview criteria to the stack of English résumés, you identify all the résumés that fit the profile you are looking for. These candidates will move on to the next step and be invited for interviews.

A Passion for Teaching

We have found that above and beyond identified needs considerations (in the English department example above, computer expertise and experience in drama), when reviewing applicants just out of school, it is best to look for some evidence that the applicant has worked with children before. This can take the form of summer camp counseling, day care work, coaching Little League, volunteering at a youth center, acting as a Boy Scout leader, and so on. These experiences are powerful indicators of who will be successful as teachers. We have found that the very best teachers are not necessarily those whose first love is their

Some Tips on Reading Résumés

Neatness counts. Consider the organization, clarity, attention to detail, format, and writing quality. These can tell you a great deal about the personal qualities of the applicant.

Look for gaps. Though not a fatal impediment for an interview, gaps in the résumé dates should be noted and the applicant questioned about them when interviewed.

Beware the two-year danger sign. Be wary of candidates with former teaching positions held for two years or less. Most districts make tenure decisions in the second year. This is a sure sign of danger.

Note the frequent movers. Be wary of candidates who frequently move from district to district. This is another caution sign you should not ignore.

Read with a pencil. Make notations on the résumé in pencil. If necessary, these comments, questions, and notations to yourself can be easily erased.

Prioritize. For elementary positions and many subject areas in middle and high school, there will be an abundance of qualified candidates. Résumés that meet the interview criteria should be put in priority order.

Beware the attachments. However glowing, they are mostly solicited and contain less-than-candid information.

Look for a desire to teach. The best teachers are those who have a sincere desire to teach and love to work with youngsters.

Read the cover letter. Cover letters often reveal much about the intelligence, personal qualities, and communication skills of the applicant.

Look for names you know. Call a colleague used as a reference if you are unsure about giving an interview to the applicant.

subject matter, but those who love and care for children. They are the ones who have a real passion for teaching and working with young people. These are the ones you want. They have the "right stuff."

Attachments and Cover Letters

Let us offer a final word of caution on reading résumés. Many résumés will come to your district office or school with third party attachments. These attachments (usually letters of recommendation, testimonials, reviews) are less important than the résumé itself. Third party testimonials (all of which are solicited and nonconfidential) do not always present a complete picture of the candidate's strengths and weaknesses as a teacher. The cover letter is another matter. If read carefully, the cover letter will give you good insight into the applicant's thinking about teaching, ability to write (and think), communication skills, and overall intelligence. These are important things to consider when hiring staff. You should not consider a candidate whose cover letter is poorly written, sloppy, or badly edited.

Step 5: Forming and Training Screening Committees

The fifth step in the Supportive Supervision hiring process is *forming and training screening committees.* By using a screening committee to do the initial interviewing of applicants, you will be able to see and choose from a large pool of applicants, all meeting your initial profile, to get the right teacher for the open position. Screening committees can be a valuable resource that will not only help you see a large number of applicants, but if properly trained they can ensure that the applicants being considered meet all qualifications and are suitable for the school. Increasingly, school districts are adopting some form of screening committee method for the hiring of both teachers and administrators.

Size and Composition

The size and composition of this committee will vary according to the size of the district and whether hiring is done through a central district office, or at the school level, or some combination of both. Classroom teachers may be part of the screening committee, and in some cases there will be community representation, as well. Parents and students can play a role in the selection process for new staff and should be welcomed as viable stakeholders in this process. The growing influence of state mandated School Advisory Councils (SAC) may play a role in selecting staff in some districts, too. Whatever the local situation, an initial screening committee should be established early and chaired by one of the school's instructional leadership team members (department chairperson, assistant principal, curriculum specialist, coordinator, etc.). We have found that a committee of at least four members and no more than seven works best for the initial screening of candidates. A committee smaller than four does not have a sufficiently broad range of viewpoints to ensure the right candidates will be chosen, and a group larger than seven becomes unwieldy and will rarely agree on anything.

Teacher Representation

It is good practice to have teacher representation on the screening committee. It is best to take the initiative and invite the teacher you would like to have on this important committee. You should consider carefully and ask a teacher from the same subject area or grade level as the open position. Having a teacher (or teachers) on the screening committee has several benefits. As you interview each of the candidates, the teacher member can provide additional subject area expertise from a somewhat different and often invaluable perspective (the classroom). In addition, being on the screening committee can be a powerful professional development experience for that teacher. Finally, the screening committee experience can be a productive training ground that you can use for the development of future administrators. Finally, and perhaps most important, inviting teachers to be part of the committee gives them a greater sense of ownership for the candidate's success.

Training the Committee

Merely setting up a screening committee to do an initial interview of candidates will do little to ensure that the "right" teachers are selected to work in your school. You must not only form the committee and appoint the chairperson, but you must provide training for them to do a successful job. This is crucial. That training can take the form of a brief workshop after all members have been chosen. As is the case with any committee, it is important to charge committee members properly so that each person understands what he or she is to do. Emphasize to the screening committee that they are not hiring anyone at this point. Explain that this is a *preliminary* step in the *process* of hiring a teacher. At this stage your screening committee should be choosing those who have the potential to be hired. Certainly a knowledge of content and teaching methodology is important, but beyond this they should be looking to see if the candidate has the "right" stuff, the character, desire, attitude, personal qualities, and potential to become a great teacher.

In addition to an explanation of the committee's charge, the training session should feature at least four other items on its agenda: a quick review of the teacher profile based upon the interview criteria and special needs of the position to be filled; a thorough discussion of the culture and mission of the school so these ideas will inform both the types of questions asked and the decision making itself; specific details about the interview format, design, location, and timelines; and some sample interview questions.

> ***Screening Committee Training Agenda***
>
> 1. *Committee's charge*
> 2. *Teacher profile and needs of the position*
> 3. *The culture and mission of our school*
> 4. *Interview details*
> 5. *Sample questions*

Step 6: Interviewing Candidates

While there are no standard formats, time limits, and questions for interviewing prospective teachers, a friendly and relaxed, yet carefully controlled, interview strategy works best. The tone should be businesslike, yet welcoming and warm to put the candidate and committee members at ease. This encourages interviewees to do their best in responding to questions and helps the committee in choosing the "right" teachers to move on to the next step in the hiring process, the demonstration lesson.

Time

It is best to schedule interviews of all candidates for the same position on the same day, if possible. Start early in the day, begin on time, provide copies of each candidate's résumé and cover letter to committee members, and allow no more than 20 minutes per interview. Often you will be hard pressed to stick to 20 minutes, yet we have found that this is more than sufficient time to make a decision on whether the candidate should be invited back for the next step. It is best to hold off discussion of each candidate until all interviews are completed. Aside from avoiding time problems, delaying discussion will give you a better opportunity to compare responses once all candidates have been heard.

Questioning Techniques

Just as we expect our teachers to teach with a plan, we must plan for our interviews. Specific questions should have been formulated beforehand at the training workshop. The chairperson should greet the candidate, introduce the members of the screening committee, and ask an initial "softball" question to get the candidate relaxed and talking. For example, you might ask the candidate to tell the committee about something mentioned in the résumé that the candidate would like to elaborate upon or share additional information about. As far as possible, the same questions should be asked of each candidate. In this way you will have responses from the candidates that can form a basis for comparison.

Each member of the screening committee should have an opportunity to ask at least one of the predetermined questions. Who will ask what question should be agreed upon in the training workshop, as well. One or more of these questions should deal specifically with the culture and mission of your school. For example, you might ask each candidate how they would fit into a school culture that expects all teachers to arrive early, stay late, and make an extended professional commitment to the school, including extra help, attendance at school functions, coaching, advising extracurricular activities, and the like.

> **Some _Do's_ and _Don'ts_ on Interviewing**
>
> **Do** stick to a time schedule
> **Don't** go beyond 20 minutes
> **Don't** ask yes or no questions
> **Do** put candidates at ease
> **Do** ask similar questions of all candidates
> **Do** give nonverbal feedback
> **Do** have follow-up questions
> **Don't** forget copies of résumé for members
> **Don't** ask trick questions
> **Do** have all members ask questions

Step 7: Using Rating Scales

In the Supportive Supervision program we strongly recommend the use of a rating scale as part of the interview process. The rating scale is an important part of the decision-making process because its use ensures a level playing field. If properly done, the same criteria will be applied to all of the interview candidates in making a judgment about which teachers will be invited back for a demonstration lesson. Having each member of the screening committee complete his or her own rating scale encourages a more professional level of conversation about the candidate's strengths, weaknesses, and suitability for the position. Rating scales will help to minimize erroneous or superficial judgments about interview candidates that are based solely upon a whim or intuitive feelings or a hunch. In addition, they help protect against lawsuits based upon discriminatory hiring practices.

It is best to have screening committee members complete the rating scale form immediately after the candidate leaves the room while the memory of what was said during the interview and the overall impression of the candidate remain fresh. Waiting to complete the form until all the candidates have been seen will often result in confusion, misinformation, and vague responses. You should wait to have any meaningful discussion of the candidates, however, until all the candidates have been seen. We have found that the suitability and strength of a particular candidate is most accurately seen against the context of the entire group.

The Form to Use

A good rating scale should have a series of items delineated with a scale of values attached. The form should include items related to content knowledge, communication skills, an understanding of education, instructional methodology, professional commitment, and personal qualities. Similar to the five-point rating scales we recommend for use in the observation and evaluation process, a five-point scale works equally as well here. Numbers or letters can be used to indicate the scale of values for Excellent, Very Good, Good, Satisfactory, and Unsatisfactory. There should also be a place on the form for interview committee members to make comments about the candidate. As you can see with the sample form provided, an overall rating of the candidate is recommended, as well.

The Overall Rating

The overall rating is *not* the average of the categories, but a holistic value based upon the total performance of the teacher candidate during the interview. Some categories will weigh more heavily than others in the overall rating, depending upon the subject or area of the open position and any special needs that were identified earlier. For example, suppose the new teacher you are seeking to hire is scheduled to teach in the Advanced Placement (AP) science program. Ms. Jones, who has a very strong background in the chemical and biological sciences, is interviewed and is extremely knowledgeable but scores poorly on teaching methodology. Despite this apparent weakness, she will still rate very high in the overall rating because knowledge of subject matter is paramount for this position. Those candidates who receive the highest overall rating during the interview should be invited to do a demonstration lesson, the next step in the hiring process.

Step 8: Demonstration Lessons

Step 8 in the Supportive Supervision hiring process is inviting candidates to perform demonstration lessons. Although it can be a time-consuming process, this is without a doubt one of the very best ways to determine who is the right person for the job. During a demonstration lesson it becomes quite apparent who can teach and who cannot, who has real potential to become a great teacher and who does not. The number of demonstration lessons you observe will vary widely depending on the time you can devote to the task and the number of candidates you find suitable during the interview process. Despite the number, we have found

Figure 3.1   Rating Scale for Teacher Applicants

Candidate _____ Position _____

Committee Member _____ Date _____

On each area you are able to judge, rate the candidate:

       1. Excellent   *4. Satisfactory*
       2. Very Good   *5. Unsatisfactory*
       3. Good

                                               Comments

Academic Background ----------------------->   ___   _____
Knowledge of Subject Field ------------------->   ___   _____
Teaching Methodology ----------------------->   ___   _____
Knowledge of Education --------------------->   ___   _____
Professional Commitment ------------------->   ___   _____
Communication Skills------------------------->   ___   _____
Human Relationships------------------------->   ___   _____
Desire, Passion for Teaching----------------->   ___   _____
Warmth, Caring Attitude -------------------->   ___   _____
Initiative, Enthusiasm for Learning -------->   ___   _____

Overall Evaluation ----------------------------- >   ___   _____

Comment on Overall Evaluation _____

_____

_____

_____

that it is worthwhile in the long run to have *all* of the strong candidates perform demo lessons for each open position.

Preparing for the Demo Lesson

The chairperson of the screening committee should make all the arrangements for the demonstration lesson, including contacting the candidate with the particulars of the lesson, its time and place, and securing the permission of the regular classroom teacher. Each candidate for the open position should be asked to do a similar demonstration lesson with students in a similar type of class so that the evaluation of each candidate's performance is equitable. For example, if the open position is a regular fourth grade position, you might ask each candidate to do a reading/ writing lesson on dinosaurs to a mixed-ability fourth grade class. Or, for that health education position, you might ask several candidates to teach a lesson on the dangers of smoking.

Observing the Demo Lesson

If at all possible, two or three professional members of the screening committee should observe the demonstration lesson. This will provide a better evaluation of the candidate's performance, and it will encourage a more thorough discussion of the candidate's potential as a teacher. After introducing the guest teacher to the class, the regular teacher should leave so as not to distract the students. During the observation, sit where you can observe both the students and the teacher, and take notes for later discussion with your colleagues. Although the quality of the lesson's design and how effectively it is developed is important, far more important is observing how well the candidate interacts with the students. Content knowledge, good teaching methodology, and sound lesson planning can be taught. Try to find evidence during the lesson that the candidate exhibits positive values and a love of children. Look for an engaging personality, sincerity, warmth, and positive human interactions. These are the things that matter most.

Step 9: Decision Making

After all the interviews and demonstration lessons have been completed, it is time to make a decision about whom to hire. At this penultimate step in the Supportive Supervision process, the chairperson of the screening committee should meet with members who observed the demo lessons. The purpose of this meeting is to decide upon a ranked list of candidates recommended to hire for the open teaching positions. At this meeting it should be fairly easy to decide upon the best candidates, those who did best in the classroom. However, sometimes all the candidates will do adequate demonstration lessons and making a decision will be more difficult. More likely, the quality of the lessons, the teaching skills, and the personal interactions of the candidates will vary widely, and it will be an easy task to decide upon a ranked list. Unfortunately, there will be occasions where none of the candidates are acceptable, and you will find yourself back at Step 4—looking at résumés again. Assuming this is not the case, a ranked list should be drawn up with the names of those candidates the committee recommends hiring for the open teaching positions.

Committee Recommendations

It should be clearly understood by all members of the screening committee that this list is a *recommended* list to hire. In most cases neither the screening committee nor its chairperson has the authority to hire anyone. While laws regarding the hiring of staff vary widely from state to state and from district to district, it is usually vested in the office of the superintendent or a designee.[17]

There are often times when circumstances occur that preclude the hiring of the committee's recommendation. There are occasions when, after meeting the committee's recommended candidate, the principal or the superintendent for whatever reason chooses not to offer employment to that person. Under NCLB, the final choice must meet the new federal requirement for being "highly qualified" in his or her respective state. You must emphasize to your screening committee the importance of their work even in the event that someone they recommend is not hired.

Step 10: Pre-Teaching Training Program

The last step in the Supportive Supervision model provides training and support for that new teacher before actual teaching begins. Research shows that more than 9% of teachers leave the profession in the first year of teaching, and another 30% or more leave in the first five years. It should come as no surprise that the problem of retaining good teachers is even greater in our inner-city school systems where support for mentoring programs and professional development are often inadequate. Studies have also shown that a sound mentoring and teacher induction program will do much to retain teachers. In one such study, 97% of the mentored teachers were active in the profession one year after participating in the program as compared to 71.5% of nonmentored teachers.[18]

Induction

Merely assigning mentors to work alongside beginning teachers will not in and of itself provide these novice teachers with the teaching skills and support they will need for success in the classroom.[19] We strongly advocate the implementation of a multi-year induction program for new teachers, including a collegial mentoring component and a targeted staff development program for identified needs. Well-matched mentors, curriculum guidance, collaborative lesson planning, peer observation, and inspired leadership all should be in place to support new teachers.[20] It is important to provide a collegial process that both trains and supports new teachers from the first day of school through the first two or three years of teaching. While costly, reduced teaching responsibilities for both mentor and new teacher is an option that has gained some acceptance. Recognizing the need to retain teachers, many states have adopted induction mandates. According to a recent study by Recruiting New Teachers (RNT), seven states have induction mandates with funding, 10 states have a mandate without funding, and 10 states have funding but no mandate. Robinson (1998) reports that in 1996, 28 states had mentoring programs for beginning teachers and that 14 states have mandated and at least partially funded new teacher induction or mentoring.[21] Each supervisor should consider all of these as options for providing new teachers with the opportunity for success. Just as there is not just one way to teach children, there is not just one way to help teachers be successful.

A Good Start

The first step in that induction program begins before that new teacher steps foot into the classroom. We have found that a pre-teaching training (Pre-TT) program will do much to help that beginning teacher get off to a good start in the classroom. In a certain sense you have invested much administrative capital in finding and hiring what you hope is the "right" teacher for the job. Your first task in protecting that investment against failing in the classroom is to thoroughly prepare that new teacher for the difficult and often overwhelming job of teaching children. Those teachers who you have hired with prior teaching experience can benefit as well from a Pre-TT program as they gain a better understanding of the district's culture, the mission of the school, and its expectations for success.

Four Parts of Pre-TT

In the Supportive Supervision model, the Pre-TT program lasts from three days to a full week and contains four components: an introduction to the district; a tour of the school, the campus, and facilities; a group discussion of the district and school's philosophy, culture, expectations, and mission statements; and a series of smaller workshops on classroom management, attendance procedures, lesson planning, testing and grading policies, parent interactions, and extra curricular activities:

- *District orientation:* A morning breakfast set aside to formally welcome all beginning teachers and staff members to the district is an enjoyable way to begin. The superintendent of schools and both district and school administrators should be given the opportunity to address the assembled teachers and share their welcoming comments. A positive tone that anticipates each new teacher's success and light engaging remarks should be stressed at the welcome.
- *Group tour:* Following a breakfast welcome, lead new teachers on an extensive tour of the district buildings, grounds, and facilities. Doing so fully acquaints new staff members with the physical environment in which they will work, the community, and all of the resources available to them as teachers. In this way new staff members will be encouraged to use school and district resources and facilities that they may not be aware of or may not be in their immediate environment.
- *Group discussion:* The second day of the Pre-TT program should begin with a large group discussion of the educational philosophy and culture of the district and school. This discussion should include an examination of the district's and school's mission statements, school goals and objectives, long-range plans, and any other important documents that provide direction for the school community and inform the philosophy and culture of the school. Other discussions may center around major challenges, issues, and educational initiatives. An explanation and discussion of the professional expectations (EPC) of each school should be included, as well.
- *Seminars and workshops:* Following these large group discussions, several more narrowly focused workshops or seminars should be planned. Depending upon the circumstances of the district, its size, and the resources that are allocated for the Pre-TT program, one to three days of workshops should be planned. It is here that the mentoring of new teachers begins. Workshops should be of two varieties, general workshops for all new teachers and workshops that are subject-area specific. In the general type, workshops should be offered to new teachers on maintaining student records and attendance procedures, learning successful classroom management techniques, understanding and enforcing the school's discipline policy, managing time effectively, establishing a testing and grading policy, utilizing the guidance and pupil resource services,

and other administrative procedures. The administrative team in each school should conduct these workshops. The area-specific workshops should be led by the area supervisors, department chairpersons, curriculum specialists, and/or teacher mentors. These workshops (or small group meetings, depending upon the number of new teachers hired in that subject area) can vary in number, but should include ones relating to lesson planning, reviewing curriculum, instructional methodology, use of technology, and best practice.

SUMMARY

As we have seen, hiring the right teachers for your school is a daunting challenge. The time you spend recruiting the right teachers, interviewing many candidates, and observing demonstration lessons is important and productive time that has immeasurable benefits. As a supervisor you recognize that your most precious resource is your teachers. As the "right" teachers begin to instruct and work with the children in your school, you will be building a culture and environment of success. You will be leading a staff of professionals who place both the personal and the academic needs of children first. These are the teachers who are committed to their own professional growth and development and to the success and welfare of all children. You now have the right teachers on board and after a successful Pre-TT program are off to a good start. You are now ready to begin the full Supportive Supervision program.

Goal Setting

Goal Setting is the *first* order of business in the Supportive Supervision program. It appears at the top, or the first position, in the continuum because it both begins and ends the process of Supportive Supervision. Goals are both established at the beginning of the school year and evaluated at the end. As the continuum indicates, in this chapter we discuss how to set goals, how to examine data to create objectives and strategies, and how to evaluate them. We also offer specific examples of goals and objectives and provide a template that can be used to organize each element in the goal setting process.

THE NEED TO PLAN

Establishing clear and sensible goals and objectives has gained wide acceptance as a supervisory and management tool in practically every large organization, including schools.[22] As in all institutions that involve intricate human interactions, managing what occurs in a school is a complex task. We recognize that in the business world a company needs a clear mission and a sound business plan to find success in the marketplace. Wal-Mart grew from a single dime store in a hardscrabble cotton town in upstate Arkansas into the world's largest business and the world's largest employer with a well-thought-out and carefully focused business plan. From the beginning it understood what its business plan would be (buy in bulk and sell for less) and where it would do business (small or secondary markets overlooked by large retailers).[23] If we look at schools in a similar way, as organizational entities providing a service, the same principle applies. In order to be successful in providing a quality service (education) to its clients (students), schools, like all social, government, and business organizations, need a clearly focused and well-thought-out plan. This has become increasingly important as we respond to the challenges of the federal NCLB legislation. For example, NCLB provides each district and school that falls below the standard with Adequate Yearly Progress (AYP) targets that must be met.

SETTING THE GOALS: A COLLABORATIVE PROCESS

As we have seen in Chapter 1, goal setting is a crucial first step in the Supportive Supervision program. It is essential that you work with your staff each year to establish goals. You should not only set personal goals for yourself as a supervisor, but you should work *collaboratively* with your staff to establish goals and objectives. Elementary and middle school principals should work with department and grade leaders and/or teachers in setting the goals for the year, while high school principals and administrators should work with individual department heads and/or curriculum-area specialists. Finally, all department chairpersons should work collaboratively with the teachers they supervise in planning goals and objectives. Although setting goals is primarily a tool of management to organize and direct the operations and functioning of the school, it should be a collaborative process, a team effort, developed with input and the support of the entire staff. The dialogue you initiate and develop with your staff about goals is vital for your success as a supervisor. All staff must have real input and a significant role in developing these goals and objectives. Staff members often resent goals and objectives imposed upon them without input and true collaboration, and in the end such an authoritarian, top-down approach is largely ineffective. A team process and a genuine collaborative effort will encourage a broad ownership of the goals by everyone, making it more likely that all staff members will "buy into" the program and strategies that will be implemented to achieve those goals.

Set Goals at All Levels

In the Supportive Supervision program goals should be established at each level and for each staff member within the academic structure of the school. In other words, there are goals for the entire school as a whole, for its individual departments or grades, for the administrative or supervisory team, and for each classroom teacher. Schoolwide goals will reflect broad educational outcomes, while individual goals and objectives will have a more narrow focus.

In our program these goals are collected, refined, and organized into an integrated, overall instructional plan for the school. In a sense, the collected goals for the school are its "business" plan for the year. With a clearly focused, collaboratively developed, sound educational plan in place, a school will have a blueprint in hand to provide educational excellence and academic success for all of its students.

Goal Types

School Goal -------------> Improve student achievement

Department Goal ------> Improve student achievement in mathematics

Individual Goal --------> Improve student achievement on the statewide math assessment

---

The Goal

Although you will often find the words used interchangeably, following the Drucker model in the Supportive Supervision program there are important distinctions between the

---

A goal is the broad, overall direction in which you want to go. It is a global educational outcome or the general change you wish to effect.

---

terms *goal, objective,* and *strategy.* A *goal* is defined as the broad, overall direction in which you want to go. It is the general educational change you wish to effect. Traditionally written as infinitive phrases, goals are often global in nature. Examples of goals for an entire school might be "to improve student achievement," or "to encourage greater parental involvement."

That broad educational direction provides the starting point for the departments or grade levels as they establish and develop their objectives. In using the example of the goal "to improve student achievement" cited above, the social studies department in one high school might develop its objectives around improving the passing rates in its courses, while the English department might seek to improve student performance on the

State English Language Arts Exam. The physical education department might seek to improve student participation in its sports program, while the school library might want to increase book circulation or classes taught. An elementary school might want to improve reading or math scores in Grade 4 or offer additional lab time for students in the science program. All these objectives are focused upon the overall goal of increased student achievement. The Goals text box at the bottom of

---

Goal ------------> *to improve student achievement*

Objectives   Improve passing rates in all social studies courses
Improve student outcomes on State Language Arts Exam
Improve student participation in sports
Increase book circulation
Improve Grade 4 math and reading scores
Increase science lab time

the preceding page illustrates how these objectives (in an abbreviated form) all support the overall goal.

These objectives are clear statements of purpose, but they are incomplete objectives. As we will subsequently show, in the Supportive Supervision program objectives must have a *measurable, quantifiable* component to be fully realized.

Goal Setting for Everyone

In the Supportive Supervision program we recommend that goals be established for all individuals in the school, including supervisors. Chairpersons, grade leaders, and classroom teachers will have individual responsibilities directly tied to the academic objectives that are established for their respective departments, whereas goals for the administrative team may reflect additional concerns relating to the functioning of school as a whole, the student body, the parents, the faculty and support staff, or the community. For example, a goal for the principal might be to improve parent involvement in the school. Objectives might be written to target increased PTA membership, the increased use of school volunteers, improving attendance at school events, or improved communication with parents. Another may involve increasing the quality and number of contacts with community leaders and organizations.

> **Principal**
>
> Goal ------------> **Improve parental involvement**
>
> **Objectives:** Increase parent and staff membership in PTA
> Increase community participation in school events
> Increase parental communication
> Increase use of parent and community volunteers
> Increase contacts with community leaders

As was the case above, these objectives will need a quantifiable element to complete them. Other goals of the principal will often relate to providing staff development opportunities and programs. Assistant principals might seek to improve discipline procedures, increase communication with the staff, or increase student participation in the extracurricular program.

By their very nature, goals are very broad, global educational outcomes. Goals are the essential starting points that require refinement, an analysis of data, and much more careful thought if they are to be achieved. Establishing these broad educational outcomes, or goals, is the first "giant" step in the Supportive Supervision process of goal setting.

DATA ANALYSIS

Writing specific, measurable objectives based upon the goal is the next step. Without objectives to target and measure their achievement, goals are empty phrases, mere platitudes, or wishful thinking. If the overall goal for a school is "to improve student achievement," without being accompanied by a well-thought-out, carefully written set of specific objectives, any improvement in achievement will be hard to measure. Without concrete, measurable objectives, it will be difficult to see if any achievement has, in fact, occurred at all.

Look at the Data

But before you can formulate the more specific objectives that will measure whether you have achieved the goal you have set, you must look at the educational *data*. Data analysis is the all-important process stage between establishing goals and formulating objectives. In fact, it is only through an analysis of data that workable and appropriate objectives can emerge. Data can be defined broadly as *all the necessary and important information* that is associated with the goal. Educational data are usually expressed in mathematical form as statistics.

> *Usually expressed in mathematical form as statistics, <u>data</u> are all the necessary and important information that is associated with the goal.*

Examples of Data

Educational data can take many different forms because schools are extremely complex cultural and physical environments. There is almost a limitless range of things that can be looked at mathematically and expressed as data in a school. Data can be as significant as the number of high school graduates attending four-year colleges, to the more mundane percentage of working toilets. Because schools are fundamentally institutions of learning, everything that occurs in a school is in one way or another related to learning. However, it is sometimes helpful to differentiate educational data into two distinct types: *testing data* and *other educational data* directly or indirectly related to student achievement. For example, the percentage of students in Grade 9 passing Spanish I would be considered testing data, while the number of students arriving late to school on Mondays, although clearly related to student achievement, would be considered other data.

Types of Data	
Testing Data	*Other Educational Data*
State exams	Attendance figures
Course grades	Drop-out rates
Proficiency exams	Enrollment statistics
Standardized tests	Number of referrals
SAT exams	Suspension rate
Item analyses of tests	Library circulation
Passing percentages	Number of parent visits
Final exams	Number of counseling sessions
IQ tests	Teacher-student ratio
AP results	Demographics
Graduation rates	

Testing data can include test results on standardized tests, state proficiency exams, SAT exams, or course grades. Subject area test grades given within the school; passing percentages on final exams; failure rates for courses, programs, and tests; and item analyses of test questions are also considered testing data. Other kinds of educational data can include demographic breakdowns, attendance figures, drop-out rates, library circulation totals, course enrollment statistics, number of parent visitations, teacher and student attendance patterns, or student percentages of one sort or another.

The Three-Year Rule

In order to identify trends in the educational data, *at least three to five years* of statistics are needed. You will find it difficult to adequately gauge what would be an appropriate and achievable objective based upon an analysis of a single year of data. Looked at in isolation, any one year of data can be an anomaly. To obtain a clear picture, you should look for *trends* in the educational data. By analyzing at least three years you are better able to judge whether the results are improving, declining, or remaining steady. For example, suppose you are looking at the test scores on a state reading test to establish an objective for your eighth grade class. You look at last year's test results, and you find that 20% of students scored in the highest reading achievement level. You want to improve on that percentage in the top level so you establish as the reading objective for the eighth grade to increase that percentage to 25%. You are satisfied with that objective, but a closer look at the data shows it to be an inappropriate one. Looking at three years of data, you find that the percentage of students scoring at the top level has been in a sharp declining trend (50%, 38%, 20%). Rather than merely adding a 5% improvement figure as an objective, with this new information based upon three years of data, you would have identified a very serious problem and would be in a better position to establish a higher benchmark (perhaps 35%-40%) and a much more comprehensive program of strategies to achieve it.

OBJECTIVES

> Driven by three to five years of data, written *objectives* establish a quantifiable standard to measure the goal's achievement.

In the Supportive Supervision program, objectives should be established only after at least three years of data are analyzed. It is by the careful analysis of data associated with the goal that we begin to develop the objectives to meet it. *Objectives* must always be data driven and carefully focused on effecting the overall change (the goal) you want to achieve. Objectives are measurable and are always expressed as quantifiable statements of intent.

Figure 4.1   One Versus Three Years of Data

Looking at One Year of Data

Goal ----------> *to improve student achievement*

Data   **Objective**

2003 20% in top level   To increase percentage of students scoring in
                                     top level of the 8th grade State Reading Test
                                     to 25%

Looking at Three Years of Data

Goal ----------> *to improve student achievement*

Data   **Objective**

2001 50% in top level   To increase percentage of students scoring in
2002 38%   top level of the 8th grade State Reading
2003 20%   Test to 40%

Some Examples of Objectives

It will be helpful in understanding the important difference between a goal and an objective to consider a few more examples. Suppose that after collaborating with your administrative and supervisory teams, you, as a principal in a high school, establish "to improve student achievement" as one of your overall goals for the entire school. An appropriate objective based upon that goal for the English department might be "to increase the passing percentage on the district final exams by 4%." The music department might want to "increase the number of students continuing with its elective program by 100 students," while the library might seek to "increase the number of classes taught by 10%." Each department has written specific, measurable objectives after an analysis of three years of data, and each was established in line with the overall school goal of improving student achievement.

Other examples can be used to illustrate the differences using an elementary school setting. Suppose that after collaboration with appropriate staff you establish as one of the overall goals for the school to "improve student achievement in science." Based, again, on an analysis of at least three years of data relating to science test scores and science achievement, you might set an objective in Grade 5 "to increase passing rates on all science exams by 10%." In Grade 4 you might seek to "increase the

Figure 4.2   High School Objectives

High School Objectives

Goal ----------> to improve student achievement

Data		Objectives
2001	88%	Increase passing % on district final exams by 4% (Eng.)
2002	89%	
2003	89%	
2001	712	Increase the number of students continuing in the
2002	689	music elective program by 100
2003	680	
2001	401	Increase the number of classes taught in Library by 10%
2002	396	
2003	390	
2001	90%	Improve passing % in all Phys Ed classes by 4%
2002	90%	
2003	88%	
2001	8%	Increase percent of students in Grade 10 on Honor
2002	9%	Roll to 20% of class
2003	12%	

---

number of science lab lessons by 20%," while in Grade 6 you might "increase student participation in the District Science Fair by 20%."

A Benchmark

In both the high school and the elementary school examples cited above, the objectives are written with mathematical targets, or benchmarks, to measure whether the goal of improved student achievement has occurred. Because they are *quantifiable* statements of intent, objectives provide a way to measure how much (or how little) success is achieved in meeting the goal. If objectives are written without a quantifiable component, or a measurable target, it is difficult to accurately determine if the goal was achieved. In fact, without quantifiability the objective may be achieved with little effect on meeting the overall goal. For example, if the elementary objective in Grade 4 above was written without a quantifiable

Figure 4.3   Elementary School Objectives

Elementary School Objectives

Goal ----------> to improve student achievement in science

Data		Objectives
2001	28	Increase the number of science lab lessons by 20% (Gr. 4)
2002	30	
2003	33	
2001	78%	Increase passing % on science exams by 10% (Gr. 5)
2002	79%	
2003	82%	
2001	40	Increase participation in Science Fair by 20% (Gr. 6)
2002	38	
2003	38	

---

benchmark, as "to increase science lab lessons," the objective could have been met by an increase of one additional lab, yet experience tells us that this would have little or no impact on the goal of improved student achievement in science. For educational objectives to be valid and workable targets, we believe they should be expressed in quantifiable terms.

THE STRATEGY

After at least three years of data have been analyzed and measurable objectives are formulated, you are ready to create specific actions, or *strategies*, that will affect the outcome.

> Assigned to specific personnel, *strategies* are specific actions designed to achieve the objective.

Strategies are specific actions or a series of actions that are designed to achieve an objective.

Similar to objectives, effective strategies must be very specific in nature in the Supportive Supervision program. Although they need not be expressed in mathematical terms, as objectives need to be, strategies should be specific to be objective. More important, strategies need to be *time valued,* and *assigned.* In developing strategies, specific personnel should be identified who will be responsible for their implementation. Completion dates for strategies should be established as well.

Figure 4.4   High School Objectives and Strategies

High School Objectives and Strategies

Goal ----------> to improve student achievement

English

Data	2001 88%; 2002 89%; 2003 89%
Objective	Increase passing % on district final exams by 4%
Strategy	Develop departmental mid-term examinations modeled on district finals

Music

Data	2001 712; 2002 689; 2003 680
Objective	Increase the number of students continuing in the music elective program by 100
Strategy	Give extra help sessions before school to all beginning music students

Library

Data	2001 401; 2002 396; 2003 390
Objective	Increase the number of classes taught in Library by 10%
Strategy	Coordinate with the academic teams in Grades 9 and 10 on interdisciplinary projects

---

Some Examples of Strategies

Continuing with the examples cited above, a strategy to effect the music department's objective of increasing "the number of students continuing with its elective program by 100" might be to have all instrumental music teachers give extra help sessions. The English department might form a committee of its members to develop mid-term examinations to meet its objective of "improving test scores on district finals by 4%," while the school library might direct the media specialists to work with academic teams on interdisciplinary projects to meet its objective of "increasing lessons taught by 10%."

In the elementary school examples, a strategy to implement the Grade 6 objective of increasing the "student participation in the District Science Fair by 20%" might be to have the science specialist hold a mini Science Fair in the fall. In order to achieve its objective of increasing "the number of science lab lessons by 20%," Grade 4 teachers might be asked to do more hands-on science experiments, and Grade 5 teachers might use

Figure 4.5   Elementary School Objectives and Strategies

Elementary School Objectives and Strategies

Goal ----------> to improve student achievement in science

	Grade 6
Data	2001 40; 2002 38; 2003 38
Objective	Increase participation in Science Fair by 20%
Strategy	Conduct mini Science Fair in the fall

	Grade 5
Data	2001 78%; 2002 79%; 2003 82%
Objective	Increase passing % on science exams by 10%
Strategy	Employ weekly review lessons and game methodology

	Grade 4
Data	2000 28; 2001 30; 2002 33
Objective	Increase number of science lab lessons by 20%
Strategy	Do one hands-on science experiment per week

---

review lessons and games to help meet their objective of "improving the passing rate on all science exams by 10%."

In each of these examples of strategies described above, specific actions are assumed by targeted individuals or groups of individuals—music teachers, media specialists, a group of English teachers, the elementary school science specialist, the Grade 4 and Grade 5 teachers. The assigned personnel have the responsibility to implement the strategy. It is not "given" to the individual by you as the supervisor from your position of authority, but through a supportive, collaborative process within the group in which the goals, objectives, and strategies are developed; it is assigned to the person or group of persons most responsible for its implementation.

Use Multiple Strategies

A single strategy will rarely result in achieving your objective. Following Drucker, in the Supportive Supervision program we recommend that you use a multiple strategy approach. You will have a much better chance of achieving the objective and thereby meeting your goal by developing a number of different strategies. It is best to employ at least three

Figure 4.6   Multiple Strategy Approach

Multiple Strategy Approach

Goal: Improve student achievement in social studies

Data	Objective	Strategies
1998 = 15%	To increase mastery rate	1. Develop a SS Honor Roll each quarter with 85% target goal grade.
1999 = 19%	(85%+) on final exams	2. Establish 85% as passing grade in all Honors classes. Students may use make-up exams until standard is met.
2000 = 17%	to 25%	3. Form a Mentors Club of honors students to provide extra help before and after school.
		4. Use mastery learning techniques on all SS essays and writing assignments.

---

different strategies for each objective. By using a collaborative model and team approach to goal setting, many excellent strategies will invariably emerge from the discussion and interaction of all members of the group. This dynamic collaborative process can serve as a powerful motivating tool energizing your staff to even greater achievement. Figure 4.6 illustrates how multiple strategies can be developed from a single objective.

As you can see in Figure 4.6, a variety of policy, program, and instructional strategies are employed to achieve the 85%+ objective: the establishment of a social studies Honor Roll and a Mentoring program, a raising of the standard passing rate, and the employment of mastery teaching techniques. What remains is the identification of the person(s) responsible for the implementation of each strategy, completion dates, and a mechanism to evaluate its achievement.

EVALUATION

The last step in the Supportive Supervision goal setting process is evaluation. It is essential that all goals be evaluated to determine if they have been achieved. Goals and objectives become just theoretical statements of intent without careful evaluative instruments. Without a way to assess achievement, objectives cannot be adjusted or modified to reflect changing circumstances. In addition, it is difficult to monitor the progress you have made toward achieving the objective without some form of evaluative instrument in place.

Assessment processes are apparent everywhere in a school environment, including the classroom and the athletic field. Just as teachers evaluate the academic achievement of their students by giving tests and coaches test the athletic skills of their players by staging games, we must evaluate the goals and the objectives we set. In the Supportive Supervision program, evaluation works from the bottom up. It begins with carefully selecting a method of evaluation (MOE) each time you devise a strategy. Evaluative instruments vary widely and you will find several to choose from, so the MOE you select as you develop the strategy should be the one that best monitors its achievement.

An MOE Example

An example of an MOE from the social studies goal cited in Figure 4.6 will make this point much clearer. With the first strategy of creating "an SS Honor Roll each quarter with 85% target goal grade" we would look for an evaluative instrument that would best monitor student grades. Suppose we have several things to choose from in monitoring and evaluating that strategy. We could ask our teachers to submit individual grade reports, but that MOE would be an onerous task. We could photocopy teachers' grade books and do the analysis ourselves, but that clearly would be an unwieldy MOE. A better MOE would take advantage of the statistical reports on student grades that are generated in most school districts each quarter. These reports utilize computer technology to produce a variety of statistical data on student grades, including mastery rates (85%+). Though the hand-written reports and photocopies would work, these quarterly grade reports are the MOE that best monitors the implementation and achievement of that strategy.

GOALS FOR THE NEW TEACHER

When working with new teachers, it is best to limit the number of individual goals and objectives that are established. Because of the myriad challenges they encounter, the often huge work load they carry, and the complexity of learning how to teach, new teachers often feel overwhelmed.[24] We have found that beginning teachers are more successful and experience fewer problems adjusting to the demands of teaching when they concentrate their instructional efforts on developing basic

Figure 4.7   Method of Evaluation

Method of Evaluation

Goal: Improve student achievement in social studies

Data	Objective	Strategies	MOE
2001 = 15% 2002 = 19% 2003 = 17%	To increase mastery (85%+) on final exams to 25%	1. Develop an SS Honor Roll each quarter with 85% target goal grade	Quarterly grade reports % of students 85%+

---

instructional skills. It is a good idea to focus the instructional objectives of beginning teachers on writing sound lesson plans containing all the essential elements of effective instruction.

Sound Planning

Efficient classroom management of routines and effective lesson planning will in most cases dissipate those "discipline" problems that new teachers often encounter. It is more important that new teachers master the basics of effective lesson planning and classroom management before tackling more sophisticated things. The subtle nuances of employing reader response theory to new text, or peppering class discussions with higher level questioning techniques, for example, can wait until the basics are firmly established. While the ability to use such methodology is important in the professional growth and development of all teachers, asking beginning teachers to develop these advanced skills would be a daunting, and in most cases a frustrating, experience. It would be beneficial for new supervisors to reflect upon their own experience as beginning teachers and recall how challenging and how difficult it was to master even the most basic and rudimentary elements of teaching children well.

GOALS FOR THE MARGINAL TEACHER

Similar to the beginning teacher, it is best to use a limited approach in establishing instructional goals and objectives for the marginally competent teacher. Although it is hazardous to generalize because individuals vary so widely, we have found that most marginal teachers have a wide range of instructional deficiencies. Rather than attempting to fix everything wrong all at one time, it is best to go slow and first focus attention on the most egregious of the instructional and/or behavioral problems. Doing so creates less confusion for the marginal teacher, and helps to focus your support and resources on just one or two areas. The marginal teacher will have a better chance for success and improvement if the objectives are limited in this initial stage. This will help both you and the teacher develop the more successful instructional strategies designed to improve performance. When the teacher begins to demonstrate improved instructional competence in one area, the instructional objectives can be adjusted to include other areas of weakness.

Mr. Brown

A specific example will make this process clearer. Suppose the following scenario: You are a newly appointed mathematics supervisor. In your department is Mr. Brown, a veteran math teacher with more than 20 years of experience. Though he has excellent content knowledge of mathematics and good classroom management, his students consistently perform poorly on tests. Mr. Brown's failure rate is the highest in the department, and his students do poorly on the state proficiency test of mathematics. After several observations during the course of the year, you discern that Mr. Brown's lessons are dull and unimaginative, he is often listless and inexpressive, and the students appear bored and uninterested. What individual goals and objectives for the next school year would you establish with Mr. Brown? What will you discuss with him and what strategies will you employ? What needs to be done to help this marginal teacher improve his competence?

Like the beginning teacher, instructional goals for Mr. Brown should be limited in number, yet they must address the most serious deficiencies. In this case you find that there are two: the lack of engaging instructional activities and the teacher's lack of interest and enthusiasm. As a supervisor you can help Mr. Brown create more engaging math lessons. You can help him develop instructional activities that invite more active student participation. Some of the strategies to achieve that objective might involve Mr. Brown's observing master teachers in the department or school, videotaping portions of his own lessons, participating in team planning sessions, and attending mathematics workshops or professional development activities on new instructional methodology.

Implementing these strategies will certainly improve Mr. Brown's understanding and ability to create more successful, more engaging instructional activities. However, finding the right strategies to motivate Mr. Brown and to successfully address his lack of enthusiasm in the classroom is a far more difficult task. Open and honest communication, a supportive attitude, your expectations for his success, and a collegial relationship with Mr. Brown are key motivating factors.[25] Moreover, matching the teacher's skills and interests with instructional activities can work well in recapturing a teacher's enthusiasm. Suppose you learn that Mr. Brown loves math games and is a crossword puzzle enthusiast. Encouraging Mr. Brown to find creative ways to incorporate his love of games and puzzles into his lessons, either as short motivational "Do Nows" or longer instructional activities, will undoubtedly improve his overall animation and enthusiasm in the classroom.

PUTTING IT ALL TOGETHER

As we have seen, goal setting is the all-important first step in the Supportive Supervision program. It is the educational road map that directs and guides the delivery of all instruction in the school. This road map is a complex document with a mix of shades and colors made up of all the individual departments, grades, and subjects within the school. All the various parts, all the particular details and pieces must be clearly and consistently drawn so that everything fits together seamlessly to form a unified whole. To create this educational road map, a clearly organized and standard format should be utilized. A fully developed example of an instructional goal for a high school social studies department with all six parts might be written as shown in Figure 4.8.

For a middle school example, we have chosen a physical education goal in Figure 4.9 to illustrate that developing goals and objectives within a school should not be limited to academic subjects, but should be utilized in all academic areas.

Figure 4.8   Smallville High School 2003-2004 Social Studies Goals and Objectives

Goal: Improve student achievement in social studies

Data	Objective	Strategies	Person	Date	MOE
01 15% 02 19% 03 17%	To increase mastery rate (85%+) on final exams to 25%	1. Develop an SS Honor Roll each quarter with an 85% target goal grade.	Chairperson	Ongoing	Quarterly Grade Reports
		2. Establish 85% as passing grade in all Honors classes. Students may use make-up exams until standard is met.	Ms. Jones, Smith Mr. White, Baker, Fleming	Ongoing	Quarterly Grade Reports, Final Exams
		3. Form Mentors Club of honors students to provide extra help before and after school.	Ms. Jones, Mr. Clyde	Ongoing	Quarterly Grade Reports
		4. Use mastery learning techniques on all social studies essays and writing assignments.	All department members	Ongoing	Final Exam reports

Figure 4.9   Smallville Middle School 2003-2004 Physical Education Goals and
Objectives

Goal: Improve parental involvement

Data	Objective	Strategies	Person	Date	MOE
01 15% 02 13% 03 10%	To increase membership in Parents Booster Club by 50%	1. Publish names of all Smallville student athletes in local press before each home game	Chairperson, all coaches	Ongoing	Observation Membership totals
		2. Have all award winners and all coach's nominees recognized in school newspaper and local press.	Publicity advisor	Ongoing	Observation
		3. Utilize cheerleading squads to increase publicity at community events.	Cheerleading advisor	Ongoing	Event schedule appearances
		4. Honor a parent with a service award for dedication and outstanding community service.	Chairperson	June Awards Assembly	Nomination
		5. Recruit new parents to join Booster Club through mailings announcements, personal contact.	Chairperson, all coaches	Oct. & Ongoing	Membership totals

Lesson Planning

Lesson Planning is the second step in the Supportive Supervision program. In the continuum, Lesson Planning appears as the next item clockwise after Goal Setting, which suggests that all lessons should follow and be closely connected to the established curricular and instructional goals for the year. As the continuum makes clear, instructional planning is an integral part of our supervision program. In this chapter we will show you how to encourage your staff to use all the essential elements of effective instruction, how to foster collaborative efforts, share resources, and establish planning teams. We will also explain ways how you can "keep current," remaining aware of the most recent developments in your field, and demonstrate how you can use teaming and mentoring strategies to help beginning teachers, experienced teachers, and marginal teachers improve instructional planning. Finally, we will provide two lesson plan formats you can use as planning aids.

As with most important endeavors, teaching begins with a plan. The lesson plan is the teacher's blueprint for building learning opportunities in the classroom. It provides the framework, supporting structures, and sequences for the teacher to follow and build upon as the lesson unfolds. Though not the sole determinant for learning, a carefully designed, well organized, and detailed lesson plan is a necessary component in the process. While it is true that many other factors, including the characteristics of the teacher and motivation, influence student learning, good planning is a key to success in the classroom. It is, in fact, the essential building block of all instruction, and it begins in quiet reflection long before the bell sounds to begin class and the teacher walks into the room.

PLANNING SHOULD BE LINKED TO GOALS

As the second component of the Supportive Supervision program, lesson planning flows directly from goal setting. In one way or another, either directly or indirectly, all instructional planning should be connected to the academic goals, objectives, and strategies that were first established at the beginning of the year. In addition to building lesson plan skills, teachers should be given opportunities and encouraged to collaborate and reflect upon how best to create lessons that transform the academic goals, specific objectives, and strategies into concrete learning activities for their students.

A Social Studies Example

Using the social studies goal example from Chapter 4, reproduced here in Figure 5.1, we find that several strategies were developed to meet the objective of improving the mastery rate on final exams.

The first three of the four strategies to meet this objective are important components of the overall plan, yet they have only an indirect impact on instructional planning. These items relate more to establishing departmental programs or grading procedures than they do to instructional design or classroom instruction. However, the fourth strategy—use mastery learning techniques on all social studies essays and writing assignments—is a direct link to instructional planning and will affect the kinds of lessons teachers will write and the specific instructional choices they will use in the classroom.

In this mastery learning example, social studies teachers may wish to design lessons and learning activities that utilize writing folders or portfolios of student work. With proper use and careful teacher monitoring, portfolios can be highly effective tools in recording student progress and charting successive drafts of student essays. Other lessons may be solely devoted to teaching the writing process itself. These lessons may involve direct instruction and guided practice on essay organization, essay development, or the use of supporting data. And still other lessons and/or instructional segments may exploit the use of student writing partners or teams in drafting essays. Finally, and perhaps most important, implementing this instructional strategy on mastery learning should prompt greater

Figure 5.1   Complete Goal Sample

Goal: Improve student achievement in social studies

Data	Objective	Strategies	Person	Date	MOE
01 15% 02 19% 03 17%	To increase mastery rate (85%+) on final exams to 25%	1. Develop an SS Honor Roll each quarter with an 85% target goal grade.	Chairperson	ongoing	Quarterly Grade Reports
		2. Establish 85% as passing grade in all Honors classes. Students may use make-up exams until standard is met.	Ms. Jones, Smith Mr. White, Baker Fleming	ongoing	Quarterly Grade Reports, Final Exams
		3. Form a Mentors Club of honors students to provide extra help before and after school.	Ms. Jones, Mr. Clyde	ongoing	Quarterly Grade Reports
		4. Use mastery learning techniques on all social studies essays and writing assignments.	all department members	ongoing	Final Exam reports

inter-departmental collaboration and interdisciplinary lessons with the English department.

An eighth or ninth grade interdisciplinary social studies/language arts lesson plan on Ancient Egypt using research and writing partners, writing portfolios, and mastery assessment techniques might look something like this:

RESEARCH REPORT ON ANCIENT EGYPT

Do Now: Place the word *MUMMY* on the overhead and ask students to write down in their notebooks five facts about mummies or things associated with them. After three minutes, ask students to volunteer responses and create a map of the word on the overhead. Lead into the reading activity.

Goals & Objectives: The interdisciplinary lesson guiding question is, How can we describe the culture of Ancient Egypt? Students will integrate the knowledge and skills acquired from Social Studies and Language Arts through literature and process writing.
Students will be able to:

1. Enhance their vocabulary through knowledge of other cultures

2. Use narrative writing skills to retell stories of the ancient past

3. Use process writing skills to organize, draft, and complete a report

4. Collaborate with a writing and research partner

Materials: Printed materials on world cultures, magazines, nonfiction books, research reports, instruction manuals, writing portfolios, overhead projector

Development:

1. Complete the daily oral reading segment, "Mummies in Ancient Egypt."

2. Have students write a diary entry about the discovery of a mummy and share their writing with their research partner.

3. Explain expository writing and cite previous examples that the students have read on Ancient Egypt.

4. Display a collection of samples to study, for example, magazines, nonfiction books, research reports, and instruction manuals.

5. Brainstorm with students to develop a list of topics on Ancient Egypt.

6. Have students work with research partners on a mapping activity on the selected topic.

7. Have students write a short paragraph in their writing portfolio on what they want to know about the topic and what they would

like their readers to know. Have students exchange paragraphs with research partners and comment on them.

Summary: Have students review what was learned by summarizing the main points of the lesson.

Application: For homework have students revise paragraphs based upon comments of research partners. These revised paragraphs can be used as an outline for the research report. In subsequent lessons:

Reinforce the logical steps of an outline taught in a previous lesson and assign a date for a rough draft. Have research partners exchange rough drafts, make comments, and return. Have students rewrite drafts into final copy. All mapping activities, paragraphs, rough drafts, and final copies of the research report remain in the writing portfolio and are handed in to the teacher.[26]

YOUR ROLE IN THE PLANNING PROCESS

Translating the departmental or school goals, objectives, and instructional strategies into concrete classroom activities is not an easy task. It will require not only the skill, dedication, and creativity of your teachers, but your guidance, your expertise, and your wholehearted support, as well. In fact, your active involvement and participation in planning instruction is essential. While the regular review of lesson plans is important, your active involvement in the planning process means much more than this. It can take on a variety of forms: acting as an instructional resource and clearinghouse, leading small group planning sessions, encouraging departmental collaboration, holding one-on-one meetings, providing materials, and sharing resources. Your involvement should be personal and ongoing throughout the school year and not just be limited to paper shuffling and checklists. Without a careful program of instructional planning, the academic goals and objectives you have established will be mere wishful thinking and will in all likelihood remain unmet. Instructional planning is the next essential step in the realization of your goals.

SUPERVISORY REVIEW

In using the Supportive Supervision model, you act as an instructional leader who encourages collaboration and team approaches to instructional planning. As a teacher of teachers, you become a mentor and guide who supports these efforts. It is important to regularly review all lesson plans, identify strengths, encourage risk taking, and make suggestions for improvement. As an instructional leader, you should plan on spending a significant portion of each day working with individual staff members and academic or grade level teams in planning instruction. Working with both new and experienced teachers, it is important to go beyond a simple check that the established curriculum is being followed. You must encourage best practice, invite reflection, and teach teachers how to design effective lessons that engage all students.

Research tells us that providing opportunities for teachers to plan together and share resources is a good way to improve classroom instruction.[27] In using the Supportive Supervision model, we encourage you to use a collaborative approach to instructional planning. It is important that you develop trust among your staff members and foster positive relationships. Through your example, staff members should feel comfortable sharing ideas and teaching plans with each other. Teachers of the same grade level or teaching the same course should be encouraged not only to share lesson materials and handouts, but also to plan instructional activities and units together. It is important for you to not only create such an atmosphere of trust, collegial sharing, and professional development, but as an instructional leader, a teacher of teachers, you should be proactive and provide the time, resources, and opportunities for these professional interactions and relationships to occur.

KEEPING CURRENT

Best Ways to Keep Current

➤ Read professional journals
➤ Network with colleagues
➤ Meet with the field supervisors
➤ Attend professional conferences
➤ Take graduate and inservice courses

All professionals have a responsibility to "keep current." Just as doctors and lawyers must be aware of the latest research and thinking in their respective fields, so too as educators we must do the same in our field. In modeling this professional behavior, encourage all your teachers to become aware of current research and thinking in your field and help them understand what is the very best, most effective methodology to use in the classroom. In fact, NCLB has mandated that districts use research-based approaches to raise student achievement levels. As a teacher of teachers, you must, of course, understand and be able to teach best practice in your field. This is an ongoing task, and as is the case in all professions, this can best be accomplished by the regular reading of professional journals, networking with colleagues in your field, meeting with professors and field supervisors of teacher education, attending professional conferences and workshops, and taking inservice and/or graduate courses.

PLANNING WITH THE NEW TEACHER

All beginning teachers will need your ongoing support and guidance in the critically important area of instructional planning. It should not surprise you to learn that some will need more help in instructional planning than others. And a few will even need help in learning how to write a basic lesson plan. Individual circumstances and the student teaching experiences of your new teachers will vary, along with the quality of the teacher education programs they attended. As such, some beginning teachers will be far more prepared in content knowledge, preservice experiences, and teaching skills than others. With the advent of the standards movement and high stakes testing in virtually all states, there is increased pressure on beginning teachers to demonstrate instructional success and master teaching skills quickly. Many feel that they are not up to the task. In an address to a national conference on teacher preparation, former U.S. Department of Education Commissioner, Richard E. Riley, referenced a recent national survey that found that only 36% of all teachers said they are "very well prepared" to teach to the new challenging standards in K-12 schools.[28]

Use Regular Planning Sessions

In the Supportive Supervision model, instructional planning for beginning teachers should be placed in the context of the larger, more comprehensive induction and mentoring program. Lesson planning is an important part of that effort that should also include regular conferencing; classroom observations; mentoring; and sustained, ongoing support. In terms of instructional planning, it is best to have all new teachers meet with you on a regular, perhaps weekly basis, either singly or in small groups. If your district uses master teachers or mentors to work with beginning teachers, they should be invited to these planning sessions and serve as full partners with you in this process.

During these sessions, it is important that you establish a tone of support and collegial sharing. Beginning teachers should feel comfortable working with you. With the Supportive Supervision model, it is best to "coach" your beginning teachers into mastering the basics of lesson planning. As you guide them in creating dynamic and engaging lessons for their students, encourage them to take instructional risks and challenges, as well. Your new teachers must feel free to share with colleagues and to come to you for advice, for feedback, and for guidance with what worked or failed to work in the classroom. Regular communication with beginning teacher mentors is crucial. Wherever possible, form a partnership with mentors to best guide and direct the professional growth of the beginning teacher.

Teach the Basics

The weekly instructional planning sessions should encompass more than your pointing out educational resources or reviewing upcoming lessons. These sessions should carry a strong instructional component, as well. As a teacher of teachers, you should focus your efforts here on teaching the basics of instructional planning. Show your new teachers how to write fully detailed lessons containing all the essential components of effective instruction. It is important to guide them through the challenges of creating lesson plans that actively engage all students in authentic learning.

You can also address a variety of topics, depending upon the needs of the individual teacher or group. You might need to explain and demonstrate how the first few minutes of instructional time are crucial to the success of the lesson, how instructional aims must be expressed explicitly in the plan, why writing out pivotal questions will clarify intent, how to design learning activities that draw upon students' prior experience, how to incorporate summaries into lessons, how to write age-appropriate learning activities for different ability groups, how to make transitions between instructional activities, how to plan small group activities, how to estimate the timing of instructional activities, and so on.

Encourage Reflective Practice

Reflection has been found to be a powerful tool in improving teacher effectiveness. By gaining a better understanding of their own individual teaching styles through reflective practice, beginning teachers can improve their performance in the classroom.[29] To encourage beginning teachers to regularly reflect upon teaching practice, suggest the use of teaching journals, notebooks, or portfolios to record daily teaching experiences. These can be regularly shared with you and teacher mentors for input and feedback, or with others in the beginning teacher group. Using personal histories, dialogue journals, and small and large group discussions about their experiences will also help beginning teachers to reflect upon and improve their practices.

We have also found that encouraging beginning teachers to add commentary or written notes directly onto the lesson plan itself soon after it has been taught works as well. These notes and jottings taken with the memory of the lesson still fresh in one's mind can be a powerful reflecting mechanism. It is a simple and effective way for beginning teachers to record their thoughts on what was successful in the lesson and what activities or practices should be added, deleted, or changed in the future.

> **_Planning With New Teachers_**
>
> ➢ _Hold weekly planning sessions_
> ➢ _Teach basic lesson planning_
> ➢ _Include teacher mentors as partners_
> ➢ _Use coaching skills and be supportive_
> ➢ _Encourage collegial sharing_
> ➢ _Encourage reflective practice_
> ➢ _Review lesson plans and comment on goals_

PLANNING WITH EXPERIENCED TEACHERS

Working with experienced teachers on lesson planning in the Supportive Supervision program will be somewhat different from your work with beginning teachers. As with their new colleagues, your focus will still be instructional improvement; however, your emphasis with veteran staff will be on encouraging innovation, collaboration, the sharing of resources, and enhancing already developed teaching skills. You should seek to expand and deepen the knowledge base and teaching skills your experienced teachers already possess. You will want to develop the best in your staff, and move them to a higher level of performance by offering alternative methodologies, modeling best practice, and recognizing and supporting your best teachers. You will want to instill a school culture that embraces new knowledge, the taking of risks, teamwork, and the desire for continuous improvement. Unlike the weekly sessions with beginning teachers, you will not need to meet with experienced teachers to plan lessons on a regular basis, unless, of course, they are in need of extra assistance. However, experienced teachers can certainly be invited to attend these weekly sessions for new teachers to share their knowledge and expertise.

Recognize Master Teachers

Those who you believe to be master teachers among your staff should be identified and recognized for their exemplary performance. This recognition can serve as a motivating device to inspire other members of your staff to excel. Studies have shown that publicly recognizing teachers for excellence has a positive effect on a teacher's self-esteem, self-confidence, and job satisfaction.[30] Recognition can have a very positive effect on master teachers, validating their extraordinary efforts and exemplary work on behalf of children and giving them added encouragement to share their knowledge and skills with others.

In addition to being given public recognition, master teachers can be given an opportunity to actively participate in the development of the instructional planning skills of their newer colleagues. They can be invited not only to share their knowledge, skills, and expertise as master planners, but also to serve as mentors for beginning teachers. Depending upon board policy, the circumstances of the district, and the resources it has allocated for this purpose, mentorship can be a formal designation with specific duties and responsibilities as part of a beginning teacher's induction program, or it can be an informal willingness or commitment from a master teacher to serve as an experienced helper or guide. In either case, it is good practice to welcome and facilitate a team approach to instructional planning with the teacher mentors on your staff as you extend the knowledge base and sharpen the skills in writing effective lesson plans with your new staff members.

Use Planning Teams

In the Supportive Supervision program, we encourage a collaborative, team approach in instructional planning. Its genesis is an open and supportive culture that respects differences and values individual contributions to the greater good. Positive group dynamics flourish in an atmosphere of trust, mutual respect, and a sincere willingness to share knowledge and expertise. Using a team approach in designing lessons need not be an elaborate staff development project. It can be a simple matter of providing an instructional focus or project and arranging the time and opportunity for a planning team to meet. These planning teams can be homogeneous in composition (eighth grade mathematics teachers, fourth grade teachers, Spanish teachers) or an interdisciplinary grouping made up of teachers across disciplines or grade levels. Teams can also be organized horizontally (across a grade level) or vertically (including multiple grade levels). Wherever possible, different types and combinations of planning teams should be encouraged and given opportunities to develop instructional activities tied to the academic goals that were established earlier in the year.

In the past decades our nation's schools have experimented with a variety of collaborative and cooperative approaches to planning and instruction. Most current major educational reforms call for extensive, meaningful teacher collaboration. The inclusion of special education students in the regular settings and the use of interdisciplinary teaming (particularly in middle schools) has prompted much of these collaborate efforts and cooperative teaching models.[31] The use of cooperative

Figure 5.2   Instructional Planning Teams

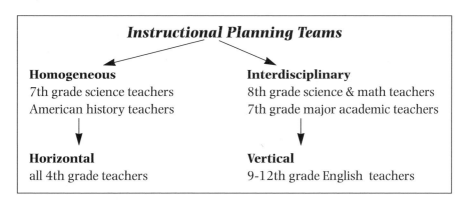

teaching and planning teams has many benefits. Teachers who have worked together see substantial improvements in student achievement, behavior, and attitude. For teachers, team planning breaks the isolation of the classroom and better prepares them to support one another's strengths and accommodate weaknesses. Teachers who work and plan together realize that they are interdependent and need to dovetail instruction to ensure they are reinforcing one another's teaching.

A Planning Team Example

The following Grade 5-6 mathematics lesson is a good example of the kind of creativity and quality in instructional planning that can result when veteran teachers from different disciplines collaborate. This lesson is the product of team planning by a mathematics and a language arts teacher.

THE MILLION-DOLLAR MISSION

Do Now: Ask students to write down in their journals what they believe are the highest salaried jobs in America and what they expect to earn with their first full-time job.

Goals & Objectives: Students determine if a 30-day payment method is better than receiving a single payment of one million dollars. To help meet the National Council of Teachers of Mathematics Standards for Algebra (multiplication and addition), Problem-Solving, Communication, Reasoning and Proof, Connections, and Representation

1. Students will be able to multiply numbers with decimals (with & without a calculator).

2. Students will understand the concept of doubling.

3. Students will be able to work collaboratively in pairs.

Materials: multiplication flash cards, pencils, calculators, student math journals, "Million-Dollar" worksheet

Development:

1. Have students review their multiplication facts using flash cards. Next, ask students, "What does one million dollars look like? What would you do with one million dollars? Today we will have a famous visitor who needs your help."

2. Have a student enter the room as "Britney Spears." (The teacher can change this visitor to any famous person that fits the interests of the students, such as a famous athlete or movie star.)

3. Have "Britney" explain to the class that she needs dancers for her upcoming event and needs the students for 30 days to assist with her concerts and the students will be paid for their help! Students are given two payment options:
   (A) Receive 1 cent on the first day, 2 cents on the second day, and double the salary every day thereafter for 30 days, or
   (B) Students can have 1 million dollars up front.

Each student must choose his or her form of payment.

4. In their math journals, students describe the situation, list the option that they have chosen, and write the reasons why they chose to receive that option.

5. Divide students into groups of two, and give each student a "Million-Dollar" worksheet. (Students will determine which payment option provides more money.) After the worksheet is completed (students may use calculators), students discuss results.

Summary: Have students review what was learned about the concept of doubling by summarizing the main points of the lesson.

Application: Have students respond to the following questions in their math journals:

Did you make the right decision—why or why not?

At what point did the doubling method exceed the flat million dollars?

When did the doubling method become an obvious difference from the million-dollar method?[32]

PLANNING WITH MARGINAL TEACHERS

Research estimates that between 5% and 20% of teachers are marginal.[33] That figure translates into 2.7 million students in the nation's classrooms who are receiving substandard instruction every day. Without a doubt, the persistence of marginal teachers is a major problem in today's schools.

Behaviors of Marginal Teachers

Marginal teachers often exhibit typical behaviors: failure to create an appropriate classroom atmosphere, lack of personal insight and motivation, and unwillingness to accept responsibility for problems.[34] A California study found similar characteristics: failure to maintain discipline, difficulties in conveying subject matter, poor relations with students, or inability to achieve desired outcomes. A 1992 survey of 135 California principals identified key factors contributing to marginal teachers' performance: lack of motivation, burnout, and personal crises. Common symptoms of teacher marginality were persistent negative attitudes and classroom control problems.[35]

The Real Problem

A sure sign of the marginal teacher—a lack of classroom discipline or an inability to control student behavior—is most often a symptom of a much more fundamental problem, poor instructional planning. There are certainly many factors that influence student behavior in the classroom (teacher attitude and expectations, delivery style, the number of students, the time of day, physical environment, school climate, etc.), yet the lack of meaningful, engaging instructional activities is often at the core of the marginal teacher's problem. "Discipline" problems in the classroom are more often than not "instructional" problems. Working with the marginal teacher on improved lesson planning will do far more to alleviate those discipline problems than arming the teacher with the latest disciplinary procedures and classroom management quick fixes.

Use a Collaborative Program

Sound lesson planning will be an essential building block in the retraining process of marginal teachers. Working with marginal teachers to improve instruction can be a challenge, yet the performance of marginal teachers can be improved with adequate diagnosis and appropriate improvement strategies, since marginal teachers, unlike those who are incompetent, are capable of reasonable performance. In the Supportive Supervision program, we recommend the use of a comprehensive collaborative program to improve the performance of marginal teachers. This program should include three components: an accurate assessment and diagnosis of instructional weaknesses, intensive training to remediate those weaknesses and improve instructional delivery and skills, and continuous feedback in the form of close observation and evaluation. For this collaborative program to have any measure of success it must occur in an environment of genuine support and trust. The marginal teacher must recognize that there are instructional weaknesses that have to be addressed. Most important, the teacher has to be willing to work with you on a program of improvement.

Using Peer Mentors

Research on marginal teachers indicates that peer collaboration can be an effective tool in the improvement process.[36] Unlike their widespread use with beginning teachers, however, using peers or mentors to coach marginal teachers can often be difficult to accomplish. Veteran teachers who are having problems often resist the idea of being assisted by mentors in the same building. Age, cultural differences, and the relationship between the marginal teacher and the mentor can be other factors that may impact the effectiveness of using mentors, as well. If not used as mentors, the master teachers on your staff can be called upon to provide instructional support in the training sessions. They can be asked to share their expertise and instructional materials and to work with you on designing training sessions. These instructional planning training sessions can be open to all members of the staff and need not be limited to marginal teachers.

Master teachers can be used in other ways, as well. While they may not have the time or inclination to be daily mentors to marginal teachers, they can be invaluable instructional resources for your training program. For example, with your master teacher's cooperation, you might ask that marginal teacher who is having difficulty in creating meaningful "Do Now" activities to directly observe the master teacher's first few minutes of class time for a week and report back to you at the next training session. The marginal teacher's notes on these observations and the subsequent

> **Planning With Marginal Teachers**
>
> *Establish a collaborative training program*
> — *Diagnose instructional weaknesses*
> — *Intensive training*
> — *Continuous feedback*
> *Utilize peer mentors*

reflection, discussion, and analysis with you can yield positive results in planning and teaching effective practice.

EFFECTIVE LESSON PLANNING

What are the essential components of an effective lesson? While not everyone agrees on a specific format and design for the planning of a lesson,[37] there appears to be broad agreement on at least most of the essential components that constitute an effective lesson. Madeline Hunter's important work in the 1960s and 1970s on effective classroom practice and instructional planning resulted in a clinical approach to the lesson plan.[38] The instructional planning concepts that she developed have contributed to most subsequent thinking about planning for the classroom, including the format and model we use in the Supportive Supervision program.

While there is no prescribed lesson plan to fit all types of lessons in all subjects, and there are many models of lesson plans in use, we believe that there are six essential components of any effective lesson: an instructional aim that is best articulated as a question, problem, or point of inquiry; a motivation or a "Do Now" activity related to the instructional aim; instructional materi-

> **Six Essential Components of Instructional Planning**
>
> AIM
> MOTIVATION
> MATERIALS
> DEVELOPMENT
> SUMMARY
> APPLICATION

als; lesson development including direct instruction, guided practice, pivotal questions, and a variety of hands-on instructional activities; a summary that reflects back on the lesson and answers the question in the lesson aim; and a lesson application or a homework assignment. Whatever the specific format or design of lesson plan your district, school, or department has adopted, these six elements in whatever guise or order should be considered when creating instructional plans. Although a sound lesson plan is no guarantee that successful instruction and learning will take place in the classroom, without it there is little chance that any real, substantive instruction and student learning will occur.

The Aim

The instructional aim is the most critical part of the lesson plan. It is the primary focus around which the lesson is organized. Depending on the type of lesson, it is often very effective to frame the instructional aim as a question or problem for students to solve. To further clarify the aim, ask what you will want the student to know or learn by the end of the lesson. The answers become a subset of the overall aim and are your instructional objectives. For example, in a lesson on teaching your seniors good interviewing techniques, your overall aim can be phrased in the form of a question: How can I make a good impression at a college interview? Your instructional objectives might be that at the end of the lesson students will learn how to smile and make eye contact, refer to their résumé, use gestures and voice modulation, dress appropriately, and so on.

The Motivation

The motivational element within the lesson can take a variety of forms. Motivation should lay the groundwork for the introduction of the aim, serving as the springboard for the lesson. This can often be accomplished by the use of an initial "Do Now" activity as students enter the room. In the Supportive Supervision model, the daily use of a meaningful "Do Now" activity as both a motivational and a transitional device maximizes the use of instructional time. Not silent busywork, a meaningful "Do Now" can act as a bridge linking your students' prior knowledge of a subject or concept with the new material that will be presented in the lesson. For example, as they walk into the room for the "Million-Dollar Mission" lesson discussed above, students are asked to write down what they believe to be the highest salaried jobs in America, or what salary they think they will earn when they get their first full-time job. Their thoughts on this "Do Now" act as a foundation of prior knowledge on which to build new knowledge. As a motivational device, this "Do Now" is designed to generate a stimulating discussion, yet at the same time it can neatly segue into the introduction to the lesson on algebraic multiplication and problem solving.

The Development

The development of the lesson requires the most time on task. All instructional activities and pivotal questions that logically and sequentially develop the lesson objectives should be described in this section of the lesson plan. In effect, it is in this section of the plan that you describe what students will be doing. In developing any lesson it is important to utilize a variety of learning activities such as demonstration, explanation, modeling, active inquiry, guided practice, small grouping, checks for understanding, and other methodologies. These instructional activities should reflect various learning modalities (visual, auditory, kinetic, etc.) as well. Finally, it is necessary that in each of the instructional activities that are planned to develop the lesson, students should be actively engaged in the learning. It is important when working with teachers to stress that students should always be seen as active participants in the lesson development, not passive recipients of knowledge.

The Materials

It is important to have teachers think about the material needs of the lesson before walking into the classroom. It is good practice for teachers to record on the lesson plan itself what materials they will need to execute the lesson. Recording and detailing everything that will be needed, collecting all materials beforehand, and testing all equipment prior to the lesson prevents the waste of instructional time. Lesson materials run the gamut of hardware and software and may include supplementary readings, physical demonstrations or props, VCR players, specialized projection equipment, paper handouts, textbooks, wall maps, computer technology, video clips, and the like.

The Summary

The summary is perhaps the most frequently underused step in instructional planning. The purpose of the summary component in a lesson is to determine whether the instructional objectives have been achieved. This is where the teacher has planned to review, recap, reinforce, and if necessary, redo the essential part of the lesson. Often the summary can review from another vantage point the lesson's basic concept, understanding, knowledge, or skill. A good summary offers the teacher an immediate opportunity to evaluate student understanding.

The Application

The application is an independent exercise or instructional activity that answers the question in the lesson's aim. It challenges students to apply learned concepts to new, related concepts, and it provides students with an opportunity to use their newfound knowledge to do additional tasks or to solve a new problem. Independent application, or the homework assignment, is work assigned to be done out of the presence of the teacher. In a well-designed lesson the best application assignments reinforce knowledge learned in the day's lesson and act as a bridge to future knowledge.

TWO LESSON PLAN DESIGNS

As noted earlier there are many types, styles, and formats that can be used to plan lessons. Whatever the format, in the Supportive Supervision program we recommend teachers use a detailed plan for each classroom lesson and that it contain all of the six essential components of instructional planning: aim, motivation, materials, development, summary, and application.

Although each emphasizes a different element, both of the following models contain all the essential components of an effective lesson. The regular use of either format will provide a useful template for effective classroom instruction. The first model developed from the work of Madeline Hunter on clinical supervision.

Figure 5.3   Clinical Lesson Plan Format

Clinical Lesson Plan Format

1. **Introduction (Anticipatory Set)**
   – Get the student's attention.
   – Relate the lesson to previous learning or knowledge.
   – State the purpose of the lesson.

2. **Objective**
   – What will the student know or be able to do at the end of the lesson?
   – How will you measure/observe that the learning has taken place?

3. **Instruction**
   – Provide information to students by demonstration, explanation, modeling, guided inquiry, and so on.
   – Check for understanding and provide additional guidance if needed.

4. **Guided Practice**
   – Allow opportunities for students to demonstrate their learning or knowledge.
   – Monitor the progress of each student, giving feedback.

5. **Closure**
   – Review, restate, recap, reteach, and reinforce the lesson, determining if each student has met the objective(s) of the lesson.

6. **Independent Practice**
   – Assign work that students are now prepared to do on their own (homework) that will enhance and reinforce the learning from this lesson.[39]

The Supportive Supervision model we offer is also a six-step approach with many similarities to the clinical approach, but uses an opening "Do Now" instructional activity as a motivational device. Our model also provides for a place to describe specific instructional materials, and to write pivotal questions.

Figure 5.4   Supportive Supervision Lesson Plan Format

Supportive Supervision Lesson Plan Format

1. **Introductory "Do Now"**
   – Use a motivational "Do Now" activity to link the lesson to students' interests, knowledge, or prior learning and anticipate instructional objective(s).

2. **Lesson Aim and Instructional Objectives**
   – State as a question the central focus of the lesson or student problem to be solved.
   – List the lesson objectives (what the students will know or be able to do at the end of the lesson).

3. **Materials**
   – List specific educational materials that will be needed.

4. **Development**
   – List all instructional activities and write out pivotal questions that logically and sequentially develop the aim and instructional objectives.
   – Check for understanding and provide additional guidance, demonstration, modeling, and so on, if needed.

5. **Summary**
   – Review main points of lesson that answer the aim question or problem.
   – Have students recap the lesson, determining if objectives have been met.

6. **Application**
   – Assign work for students to apply, reinforce, or enhance the facts, skills, and concepts learned. This can be an in-class activity under your guidance or a homework assignment.

Observation

The third component in the Supportive Supervision program is Observation. In the continuum, Observation appears as the next item clockwise after Lesson Planning. Its position here is meant to suggest that all good classroom lessons must be based on solid planning. As the continuum makes clear, observations are not isolated events but an integral part of our supervision program. In this chapter we show you how to build trust with your staff and how to adopt a positive, supportive, and collaborative approach to the observation process clearly focused on instructional improvement. We then show you what to look for in a classroom observation and how to prepare for and conduct pre- and post-observation conferences. Following this discussion, we present the Supportive Supervision observation report model. Each of its seven sections is described in detail using sample model reports.

As noted in the opening chapter, the formal observation process is a key feature of the Supportive Supervision program. Adopting our fully integrated process, you can enhance your instructional program, improve teacher effectiveness, and begin to build a great school. The Supportive Supervision observation process also serves as the foundation for improving staff development programs. Using our program will allow you to identify curriculum or program issues, build upon teacher strengths, support effective practice, and address instructional weaknesses.

A SUPPORTIVE APPROACH TO OBSERVATIONS

As a teacher of teachers, you should utilize the observation process as an instructional improvement tool within the Supportive Supervision program.

Observations are best approached as a supportive and collaborative process. Your effectiveness as a teacher of teachers is greatly enhanced by building a high level of trust with your teachers and encouraging in them a spirit of self-analysis and reflection. Teachers need encouragement, time, and a supportive climate in order to reflect meaningfully upon their teaching. As a supportive supervisor, you function as their guide, helping them to identify and articulate effective practices, validate instructional strengths, and recognize areas of weakness. As a teacher of teachers using the Supportive Supervision model, you should seek to create a positive climate of trust and respect. The ideal environment is a supportive one where teachers feel comfortable seeking your expertise and help, where they feel free to take risks in the classroom, and where they are willing to share with you both their successes and their failures. Using such a supportive approach to the observation process will help you establish an ongoing, collaborative, and professional relationship with each teacher you will be observing.

BE SUPPORTIVE WITH ALL STAFF

We do not recommend a differentiated approach to classroom observations where some teachers engage in a formal observation process while other, perhaps more seasoned, staff members are exempt.[40] Despite the number and quality of master teachers on your staff, all teachers will benefit from the Supportive Supervision observation process. This is because the primary goal in our program is the improvement of instruction and teacher effectiveness. The observation process is not about documenting classroom successes, providing teacher recognition, or supplementing teacher portfolios. It concentrates on building and strengthening a teacher's reflective practice while identifying areas where you can provide a professional development plan. Although the Supportive Supervision observation model does contain a final assessment of the lesson, it is not designed to be used as the primary evaluative instrument of the teacher, as is the case with many other observation models.[41] Even your most skilled staff will gain from our observation process because of its core focus on instructional improvement. In the Supportive Supervision program observations are a means to an end: greater academic achievement through more effective teaching.

As noted in Chapter 4, the instructional goals and objectives you establish with marginal teachers may be very different from those that you have developed with your beginning teachers. For example, a marginal teacher may need to work on improved lesson planning and incorporating more engaging student activities in the lesson, while a beginning teacher may need to work on better managing classroom routines and using a more dynamic instructional delivery. For both teachers, your approach to the observation process remains supportive: both the marginal teacher and the beginning teacher need you as a resource and as a facilitator helping them improve performance.

THE OBSERVATION PROCESS

Over the past several decades there have been a number of different classroom observation models.[42] Lately much attention has focused on peer observations.[43] However, the most widely used approach in American schools remains variations of what has been called "the clinical supervision method." Despite differences, all variants of this approach are multiphased: a planning conference or pre-conference, the actual observation of the teacher in the classroom, analyses and interpretations of the data collected, and a post-conference that focuses on reviewing the results of the observation and formulating plans for improvement.[44]

The primary Supportive Supervision model adheres to this multiphased, clinical supervision pattern. Observations are never conducted as an end in themselves, nor do they occur as isolated events or in a vacuum. Observations are not random snapshots or 45–minute script tapes of a teacher's performance in the classroom over the course of the school year. Rather, observations in our program are part of a continuous process of instructional improvement and teacher effectiveness.

Similar to the clinical supervision model, our observation process is multiphased. Four distinct phases constitute the process. Phase 1 includes a series of pre-observation practices. Whether you conduct a pre-observation meeting with the teacher during this initial phase of the

> **Supportive Supervision Four-Phase Observation Process**
>
> 1. Pre-Observation Practices
> 2. Observation
> 3. Post-Observation Conference
> 4. Written Report

process will depend upon local choice and governing policies. Phase 2 consists of the supervisor's observation and analysis of the lesson. In Phase 3 the supervisor and the teacher meet to discuss the lesson in a post-observation conference. The final Phase 4 of the process is the actual writing of the classroom observation report.

Phase 1: Pre-Observation Practices

In the Supportive Supervision program the observation process begins well before you set foot in the classroom to observe. Careful planning

---

Pre-Observation Practices

➢ Consult district policies
➢ Plan a schedule
➢ Review goals and objectives
➢ Review prior observations
➢ Conduct a pre-observation conference

---

should take place before you do any observing. As is the case with almost all aspects of teaching, good planning will be the key to your success. In our program there are five steps in Phase 1, or the pre-observation practices stage: consulting district policies, creating a plan or schedule of observations, reviewing instructional goals and objectives, reviewing prior observations, and conducting a pre-observation conference.

Know District Policy

Most districts have a large number of governing policies in place regarding the formal observation of teachers. Often, these rules and regulations, which are codified in board policy, district regulations, and official reporting forms, are a result of education law, past practice, custom, and negotiations with the local teacher organization. In these policies you will most likely find the number of observations that are required to be performed for each classification of teacher. This number is often expressed as a minimum and is differentiated for tenured and nontenured staff. For example, it is common to find that in most districts tenured staff are to be observed at least once during the school year, while nontenured staff are observed a minimum of six times. Most policies will also deal with the definition of an "official" or "formal" observation, its duration, the sequence or timing of observations for both tenured and nontenured staff members, dates for post-conferences, and other related matters. Most school districts will also use a standardized format for the final written report that will describe the kinds of data that it must contain.

You should be thoroughly familiar with all your district policies and regulations before you begin observing your staff members. It is not only important to know all the rules so that you will avoid procedural problems, but with the knowledge of what you must and must not do you can begin to effectively and accurately plan a timeline and schedule of classroom visits, observation conferences, and formal observations for your staff.

Plan a Schedule of Observations

Over the years we have practiced several observation procedures that support instructional improvement. We offer the following as general guidelines, recognizing that differences in local policies and districts will vary widely:

1. *Begin very early in the school year.* It's best not to allow the first month of school to slip by while you address other administrative details

and let teachers "settle in." It is important to get your staff off to a good start, thinking and working on their instructional goals and the use of best practice early in the school year. For beginning and marginal teachers, the third week of school is not too early to begin working with them on classroom observations. This provides much needed direction to those who are most in need of assistance.

2. *Schedule all staff observations for the fall semester.* If possible, you should plan to observe all staff members at least once during the fall semester. Because the purpose of observations in the Supportive Supervision program is the improvement of instruction and teacher effectiveness, it is important to schedule the initial observations of all staff members in the first half of the school year to allow for teacher growth and the development of skills. It is also important in developing future staff development activities because often these are contingent on needs identified during the observation process.

3. *Base master observation schedule on instructional needs of staff.* The order and sequence in which you observe your staff members should be based on the instructional needs of the school, the department, the programs, or the teachers. While teacher preference can be a factor in creating a schedule, it is more important to respond to the needs of the total instructional program. For example, it is better to observe your two beginning teachers who are working as a team in a new remedial math/science program early in the school year in order to help them shape and define instructional choices, than it is to observe that master science teacher who requests that you observe her new lab experiment on African frogs. While the frogs may be fun to watch, your time is better spent helping your new teachers.

Review Instructional Goals and Objectives

As you continue this planning phase in the observation process, you should next review the instructional goals and objectives for each teacher you plan to observe. Though it is quite early in the school year, by using the Supportive Supervision model these individual instructional goals and objectives have long been established. For all but your first-year teachers, they will have been described briefly in a section of the teacher's previous year's EOY evaluation. As you review these individual goals and objectives for each teacher you are going to observe, you should plan to discuss them with the teacher in the pre-observation conference and focus on them during the classroom observation. Be sure to reference them in the written report. For example, if one of the instructional goals written in the EOY evaluation for Mr. Bates last year was to "work on improving the use of instructional time in the classroom," you should plan to review instructional strategies that maximize instructional time during the pre-observation conference and make notations during the observation itself on how quickly the lesson began, how efficiently classroom routines were managed, and how well students moved from one learning activity to another during the course of the 45-minute lesson.

For beginning teachers, instructional goals and objectives will most likely center on the basics. Specifically, you should plan to note during the lesson how well the teacher understands and utilizes the Supportive Supervision six essential components of effective instruction: an instructional aim articulated as a question, problem, or point of inquiry; a motivation or a related "Do Now" activity; a variety of instructional materials; various lesson development activities; a summary; and a lesson application or homework assignment.

Review Prior Observations

Similar to your review of a teacher's instructional goals and objectives, it is best to review prior observations for the teacher you are about to observe. Focus on the section of the observation report dealing with recommendations. Note what these recommendations are and plan on focusing your observation on how the teacher has implemented these instructional improvements. Again using Mr. Bates as an example, suppose a prior observation of his contained this recommendation: "To improve class participation by improving questioning techniques, Mr. Bates should use more probing and more open-ended questions and avoid simple Yes or No response questions." Before you observe Mr. Bates, make a notation to look for evidence in his questioning that he has, in fact, implemented this recommendation and used more higher level questions. The successful implementation of a prior recommendation should be noted as well as the continuance of an instructionally poor practice.

By looking at prior lesson recommendations and the instructional goals that were established for each teacher before you observe, you will be in a much better position to use the observation process as a teaching vehicle to identify and address the particular instructional needs of each member of your staff. Like a successful lesson, a successful observation requires analysis, reflection, and a well-thought-out plan.

Conduct a Pre-Observation Conference

It is usually a good practice to seek an opportunity to conduct a pre-conference with the teacher before the observation.[45] The pre-conference is an excellent teaching mechanism that works particularly well with beginning teachers, who will often need lots of coaching and attention. Given a specific lesson, it is one of the key ways you can teach best practice to your staff. In certain circumstances, however, the pre-conference is unnecessary or counterproductive. This is particularly true when trying to measure the level of a teacher's preparedness.

Before the date of the pre-observation conference, request that the teacher come prepared for the meeting with a lesson plan for the class that will be observed. Stress the importance of having the teacher include all six of the Supportive Supervision essential elements in creating the plan. This then becomes the focus of your discussion with the teacher and a practical example for you to teach both your veteran and beginning teachers best practice. In many ways, the pre-conference is an excellent context for you to "teach teachers" sound lesson planning and successful instructional methodology. In the pre-conference you can tailor the instruction to the specific needs of the individual teacher.

Using Mr. Bates as an example, suppose the plan he provided in the pre-conference was not well developed. Although all six essential elements were in place and the instructional aim was very explicit, the plan did not contain any written pivotal or open-ended questions in the developmental stage of the lesson. This would be an excellent opportunity to teach Mr. Bates how to formulate pivotal questions and how these higher level questions can be used as transitional and motivational devices to fully engage students in the lesson. In working with Mr. Bates on this, you would be addressing his specific instructional needs very directly. A key focus during the subsequent observation of Mr. Bates's class, then, would be how well he used pivotal and open-ended questions to motivate students to participate in the instructional activities. The feedback he would gain from a subsequent post-conference on this aspect of his teaching performance would be very useful in helping Mr. Bates improve his skills.

Phase 2: Observation

After you have consulted policies, established a schedule with time-lines, reviewed the teacher's instructional goals and objectives, reviewed prior observations, and held a pre-conference, you are now prepared to observe the teacher's performance. You are ready for Phase 2, the observation itself. As noted above, observations should occur as early in the year as possible in order to give the teacher the maximum amount of time to learn new skills and make improvements.

In making observations, it is helpful to arrive early and try to put the teacher at ease. For the best vantage point sit in a position in the room that allows you to observe both the teacher and the students. If you have conducted a successful pre-observation conference, most teachers should experience less anxiety and nervousness at being observed. For some, however, knowing that an observation is about to occur is more stressful than not knowing. Since being observed can be a stressful experience under any circumstances for most teachers, you can minimize tension by smiling, listening attentively, and saying a few encouraging words at the beginning and end of the lesson. Be aware that your presence in the classroom may have an impact on the behavior of students; however, we have found that this impact is minimal in open and active school environments where student observers, supervisors, teaching aides, and adult visitors are commonplace.

Gathering Data

Collect as much data and information as you can in advance so that the observation can focus on events and behaviors as they occur in the classroom rather than on the administrative details. Examples of such information include the employment status of the teacher (tenured, probationary, substitute), subject and grade level, the number of students enrolled, the academic ability level (advanced, regular, special ed., etc.), the physical setting (classroom, science lab, library, computer room), student grouping (whole class, six groups of five students), the date of the observation, the start and end times of the observation, and the building and room number.[46]

During the observation it is important to keep focused on your task and function. Remember that as a supervisor you are an observer, not a participant in the lesson. Avoid the urge to "jump in" and participate no matter how engaging the activity, or to "correct" a teacher mistake no matter how egregious it seems. Correcting a mistake or challenging the teacher during the observation severely undercuts the authority of the teacher in the eyes of the students. Factual or mathematical errors, chalkboard misspellings, or similar mistakes can be communicated to the teacher during the post-observation conference.

In gathering data during the course of the observation, try to be as objective as possible, recording facts and specifics as they occur. It is a good practice to record each lesson element, sample questions, and exact quotations of what the teacher and students are saying. This would be especially important in the case of Mr. Bates where you have identified his questioning as a source of concern. Since this can be quite difficult to do as the pace of the class moves along, you may wish to paraphrase key questions and responses. We have found that it is best to refrain from making quick judgments or draw conclusions about the overall quality of the teaching or the lesson during the observation. An "early" judgment will tend to influence the kinds of evidence you record. Record both positive and negative aspects of the lesson, but avoid generalizations and conclusions at this time.

Observe With a Focus

As a supervisor, you will have a myriad of things to look at and collect data about while observing a lesson. In a successful lesson, teacher and students are engaged in a highly complex set of interactions, an academic "dance" of language, expression, and movement. In any given lesson, the teacher might be talking, asking questions, demonstrating a process, explaining a theory or a word, writing a formula, displaying a visual, moving about, pointing out items in a textbook, distributing paper, struggling with a VCR or overhead projector, directing an activity, modeling a process, and more. Students are rarely passive in this learning dance. You might observe students raising hands or responding to questions, asking questions or sitting quietly, copying notes or discussing in groups, smiling or frowning, drawing charts or writing essays, manipulating objects or observing intently, viewing a film or reading aloud, writing on the board or taking a test. In addition to these correct steps, in any lesson there are always student missteps, off task behaviors that may interrupt the dance: talking to one's neighbor, daydreaming, fooling around, and so on. So much is happening simultaneously during the course of any lesson that it is impossible to record everything. Nor would you want to. You must focus your attention and gather data on the things that matter, the essential elements in a good lesson and the things that you have identified beforehand. This is precisely why you must prepare carefully and have a focused plan before you enter the classroom.

As the lesson proceeds, make sure to take notes and gather data on the items or concerns that you identified with the teacher prior to the observation. Recalling the Mr. Bates example will help illustrate this point more clearly. Because you both have identified and discussed one major area of his teaching that needs improvement—creating and using pivotal, open-ended questions to promote greater class participation and stimulate classroom discussion—you must now make sure that you gather enough data on this aspect of the lesson. Observe Mr. Bates's questioning technique closely. It might be helpful to write down the pivotal questions verbatim as they are posed to the class, the manner in which they are asked, their frequency, and their type. Added to this data you might want to record how well the class responded to these questions, including the number of students who responded and the length of the ensuing discussion. Armed with this objective data, you will be better able to provide accurate feedback to Mr. Bates.

It is not sufficient to focus exclusively on this one aspect of Mr. Bates's lesson, however. All the essential elements of effective instruction should be noted as well. Before leaving the room, quickly check the notebooks of a few students selected at random, or the activity the students have been engaged in. This should be a rich source of data on how students understand what is being taught in the class. We do not recommend giving immediate feedback on the quality of the lesson to the teacher. It is best to just be polite and thank the teacher for the opportunity to observe the lesson. General statements on the quality and effectiveness of the teacher and the lesson are best left until later when you have had an opportunity to analyze and reflect upon all of the evidence and data that has been collected.

Observation Checklist

Because there is so much to consider during a classroom observation, an observation checklist can be an invaluable tool to help you record information during the process. Whether it is used as a prompt or guide during the observation itself or as a reflective instrument immediately thereafter, an observation checklist will ensure that you address all instructional components of the lesson, and that nothing of significance is overlooked.

Phase 3: Post-Observation Conference

It is best to conduct the post-observation conference as soon as possible after the observation itself. We have found that delaying the conference only adds to the supervisor's stress and increases the teacher's anxiety. In addition, it is important that as a supervisor you model that instructional supervision is high on your hierarchy of job responsibilities. Since we believe that instructional supervision is the most important task in the Supportive Supervision program, the entire observation process should be completed within a week's time. Just as the teacher must prepare an effective lesson plan for a successful lesson, you must prepare a "lesson plan" for a successful post-observation conference. Immediately after the observation, take time to go over the written notes carefully. With the memory of the observation fresh in your mind, add relevant details that you can recall that did not make it into the notes. Fill in the gaps and make clear the connections between the instructional strategies used and the kinds of activities that occurred. You might want to refer to the observation checklist to prompt your thinking about what occurred or failed to occur in the lesson.

After all the data have been reviewed, it is time to analyze them and formulate tentative conclusions. Specifically, you will want to examine the

Figure 6.1   Observation Checklist

Classroom management and routines

Was the teacher at the door in between classes?	Yes ☐	No ☐
Were any students late?	Yes ☐	No ☐
Did students begin working at the bell?	Yes ☐	No ☐
Did the teacher have an attendance procedure that did not interfere with instruction?	Yes ☐	No ☐
Was last night's homework collected and recorded in an organized fashion?	Yes ☐	No ☐
How did the teacher handle students who did not hand in homework?	Yes ☐	No ☐

Developing the "Do Now" motivation

What motivational "Do Now" activity did the teacher use to stimulate student interest?		
Was there a quality "Do Now" activity?	Yes ☐	No ☐
Was the motivation directly related to the aim?	Yes ☐	No ☐

Developing a worthwhile instructional aim

In what form was the aim?		_____
Was the aim too narrow or too broad?		_____
What did the teacher do to communicate the aim to the students?		_____
Did the aim reflect the required curriculum?	Yes ☐	No ☐

Developing the instructional activities

Was the teacher prepared for this lesson with a detailed, written lesson plan?	Yes ☐	No ☐
Did the lesson develop in a logical or sequential manner?	Yes ☐	No ☐
Did the teacher draw upon students' previous knowledge or readings?	Yes ☐	No ☐
What activities did the teacher provide to demonstrate student understanding of the aim?		_____
Were hands-on application exercises used?	Yes ☐	No ☐
Were students actively engaged during the entire lesson?	Yes ☐	No ☐

(Continued)

Figure 6.1 (Continued)

Was there note taking activity?	Yes ☐	No ☐
Were the notes organized?	Yes ☐	No ☐
Did the teacher utilize technology or visual aids?	Yes ☐	No ☐
Was the utilization of technology relevant to the aim?	Yes ☐	No ☐
Did the teacher provide enough activities to foster bell-to-bell teaching?	Yes ☐	No ☐

Implementing learning standards and assessments

Were learning standards identified in the lesson	Yes ☐	No ☐
Were state assessment-type questions and activities evident in the lesson?	Yes ☐	No ☐
Were these questions spiraled?	Yes ☐	No ☐
Were all students called upon to participate and to respond to questions?	Yes ☐	No ☐

Discipline and rapport with students

Were the students talking or acting inappropriately during the lesson?	Yes ☐	No ☐
How did the teacher address off-task behavior?	Yes ☐	No ☐
Did the teacher foster a classroom environment where students felt supported and nurtured?	Yes ☐	No ☐

Lesson summary

Was the summary related to the aim?	Yes ☐	No ☐
Did the summary allow the teacher to evaluate lesson objectives?	Yes ☐	No ☐
Did the lesson include an evaluative summary?	Yes ☐	No ☐
Was the evaluative summary a performance based activity?	Yes ☐	No ☐

Developing homework activities

Was the homework an outgrowth of the learning experience of the lesson?	Yes ☐	No ☐
Did the homework integrate reading and writing skills?	Yes ☐	No ☐

Continuity

Did the teacher implement recommendations from previous observations?	Yes ☐	No ☐

evidence to evaluate how well the teacher performed those indicators, behaviors, or skills previously identified and discussed with the teacher in the pre-observation conference. What evidence did you gather to show how well (or how poorly) the teacher performed? How strongly does the evidence point to success or failure in those identified areas? Is there evidence that student learning occurred in the lesson? It cannot be over-emphasized that you need to have specific documentation from the observation to support the conclusions you draw about what worked and what did not work in the lesson.

Let's use the Bates example once again to illustrate this point. Suppose you recorded the use of twelve pivotal questions during the course of the lesson, yet you noted that little class discussion ensued. The evidence showed that one or two hands were raised as Mr. Bates posed each question, and that students responded with one- or two-word answers. In addition, your notes show that of the twelve questions asked only three generated follow-up questions. This evidence suggests that something more than good pivotal questions is needed to generate more student enthusiasm and greater class participation. While you may conclude that the Mr. Bates's off-hand, lackluster manner of posing questions and the lack of spiraling questioning contributed to the poor results, it is best to lead Mr. Bates to that very same conclusion by sharing this evidence with him. By preparing a series of leading questions, you will help Bates understand the reasons why student participation was low, and why he will need to continue to work on improving his questioning technique.

In planning your post-observation conference "lesson," it is vital to include specific goals for teacher growth and development. Also include a thorough review of all the essential elements of the lesson, highlighting those that were missing or ineffective. Your plan should be a balanced one, highlighting successful items you found in the lesson as well as areas in need of improvement.

Conducting the Post-Observation Conference

An integral part of the clinical supervision method, the post-observation conference will put your skills as an instructional leader to the test. Similar to the pre-observation conference, in the post-observation conference activity your role as a "teacher of teachers" is paramount. Prepared with your "lesson plan," you should approach the conference as you would the classroom, with an overall aim, specific objectives, and pivotal questions. It is best to engage the teacher in a professional conversation about the lesson, asking leading questions to encourage self-reflection and analysis. Reflective practice can be a powerful tool to spur teacher growth and development.[47] Because the stakes are high and the focus intensely personal, the post-observation conference is perhaps the best opportunity teachers have for exercising this professional practice.

A supportive tone and attitude coupled with a positive opening remark in the post-observation conference will do much to put the teacher at ease and more receptive to the ensuing dialogue. As you would during a lesson, it is best to "ask, not tell." Avoid telling the teacher what worked and what did not work in the lesson. Rather, you should ask questions and work with the teacher so that he or she can recognize and articulate what was good and what needs to be improved. Just as important as leading the teacher through this self-reflection, you must lead the teacher to understand why an instructional practice is effective or ineffective, as the case may be. In the conference you must not only encourage self-reflection, but also teach best practice.

Some Conference Guidelines

➢ Avoid condescension or paternalism. Be a "teacher of teachers."
➢ Begin the conference with a positive remark.
➢ Focus on school/department/grade and individual goals.
➢ Have the teacher evaluate the aim and how well it was achieved.
➢ Seek commendations and recommendations from the teacher.
➢ Be a good listener, but facilitate the teacher's self-reflection.
➢ Seek consensus and agreement whenever possible.
➢ To avoid overload, limit the recommendations to 2 or 3 items.
➢ Make sure recommendations are clear.
➢ Support recommendations with specific evidence from the lesson.
➢ Provide continuity & refer to prior improvement or areas needing attention.
➢ End the conference on a positive note.
➢ Clearly discuss the rating as either: excellent, very good, good, satisfactory, or unsatisfactory.

Using the Bates example, you might pose the following pivotal questions to him as you explore his teaching performance—Which students participated in the lesson? How would you evaluate their level of participation? What evidence can you provide to support the levels of student participation? Why did this happen? Let's examine this—and so on. Leading Bates through this reflective process by the means of probing questions will result in greater self-awareness and understanding and improved performance in the future.

Perhaps the most important aspect of the post-conference is to have the teacher cite evidence of effective practices and explain why. Conversely, teachers should be asked to cite evidence of ineffectiveness, explain why this occurred, and find ways to rectify the poor practice. This interactive process in the post-observation conference not only teaches best practice, but it encourages the teacher to be self-reflective, as well.

Phase 4: Writing the Observation Report

After you have collected all the data both before and during the observation and you have met with the teacher in a post-observation conference, you are ready to put the parts together and produce a final written report. This is the fourth and final phase in the Supportive Supervision observation model. For many supervisors, writing detailed reports is rarely a task that is enthusiastically embraced. However tempted you are to put aside the writing and focus on something else, don't. We have found that it is best not to yield to the lazy charm of that familiar thief of time—procrastination. Even taking a short "break" of a few days at this point in the observation process does more harm than good. While it is important to adhere to your schedule of observations, it is even more important that you write while the memory of your observation of the lesson and the post-observation discussions with the teacher is fresh. This will help you produce a more comprehensive and balanced report.

In the Supportive Supervision model the written observation report should not contain anything that was not observed in the classroom and discussed with the teacher. To insert items of concern into the report that were not discussed in conference seriously undermines your relationship with the teacher and conflicts with the collaborative nature of the observation process. The opposite scenario—not including discussed items in the report—remains a valid strategy. For a variety of reasons, particularly concerning beginning teachers who may be struggling yet show potential, it is counterproductive to include a laundry list of recommendations and lesson deficiencies in the written report.

A Structured Essay Format

In the Supportive Supervision model, we use a structured essay format for the written observation report. Although they are popular, we have found that checklist observation formats with blank rectangular boxes for short comments are not very helpful. For an observation to be meaningful to the teacher, the essay format works best. The essay format is more flexible than a checklist, far more comprehensive, allows for greater freedom of expression, and can provide the richness of detail such an important document demands. In the writing of the report we have found that the use of the second person (you) works well to both focus and personalize the writing. The emphasis on "you" in both the descriptions and the analyses sections of the structured essay format underscores the importance of the teacher's role and responsibility as the center and the catalyst for the learning process in the classroom. In addition, a report written in the second person is written to the teacher rather than about the teacher for some other purpose.

The Seven Sections of an Observation Report

The structured essay format in the Supportive Supervision model has seven distinct sections. They are an essential data section that records the basic facts of the observation; a pre-observation conference summary, a short paragraph indicating that a pre-observation conference was held and what was discussed; a lesson description, a detailed paragraph or two describing what occurred in the lesson; a post-observation conference summary, a shorter paragraph indicating when the post-observation conference was held and what was discussed; a commendations section, several short paragraphs discussing all the positive aspects of the lesson; a recommendations section, no more than two short paragraphs identifying instructional deficiencies in the lesson with specific examples on how to improve; and a summary, a final paragraph rating the lesson, with an action plan for the teacher to implement the recommendations.

Section 1: Essential Data. The first half page of the Supportive Supervision observation report format provides space for the essential data that must be recorded regarding the observation. This includes the teacher's name, employment status, the building or school where the observation took place, the room number, the teacher's department, the grade level of the students, the name of the course, the ability level of the students, the number of students enrolled, the number of those in attendance, and the name of the observer. Space is also provided to record the important dates when the observation process occurred. In order to adhere to policy regulations and remain within deadlines, it is important to accurately record dates of the pre-observation conference, the observation itself, the post-observation conference, and the date when the written report was forwarded. Notice that the sample in Figure 6.2 includes all relevant information in a simple, straightforward format.

Figure 6.2   Supportive Supervision Classroom Observation Report (Essential Data)

SUPPORTIVE SUPERVISION
CLASSROOM OBSERVATION REPORT

Teacher's Name John Bates School Central PER 8 12:03 to 12:51

Department Social Studies Grade/Course Global Studies 10 Level R

Class Register 28 Attendance 27 Observer Ms. Supervisor

Dates: Pre-Observation Conference   11/19/03 Tenure Nontenure_X_

        Observation   11/23/03

        Post-Observation Conference   11/24/03

        Date Report forwarded   11/26/03

Section 2: Pre-Observation Conference. This section of the report describes what was discussed with the teacher at the pre-observation conference meeting. Record here a summary of what plans were discussed and any pertinent details about the upcoming observation. The section need not be longer than a single paragraph. Two representative samples of pre-observation conference summaries follow:

During the pre-observation conference, you and I discussed the instructional aims in the lesson to be observed. Referring to the Instructional Planning Report you had prepared for this meeting, you indicated that the primary aim of the lesson was to have your students review math concepts and problems for an upcoming test. To accomplish the review, you planned to have students play a "baseball" review game. We then discussed how the use of game methodology can create an exciting and sound instructional focus for a lesson. We agreed that aside from providing a general review of the topics to be tested, the students as game players would learn valuable lessons in sportsmanship and cooperation. We then reviewed the planning report and discussed how best to incorporate game methodology into the proposed review lesson.

At the pre-observation conference, you and I discussed my planned observation of your work with the Talented and Gifted students the next day. You provided me with a schedule of events and seminars for the next day's observation, explaining that the schedule of activities is flexible and that certain programs could be canceled depending upon student availability and coverage. We then discussed the activities TAG students were currently engaged in. You explained that this past year, students have written plays, acted in dramatic scenes, and discussed such varied seminar topics as dreams, subliminal influences, handwriting analysis, mind control, and stress. Other students are in the process of writing an experimental group novel, and creating a video on all TAG activities. Others are conducting debates, and participating in local and national essay contests.

Notice that both samples reveal the collaborative nature of the observation process. In both cases the supervisor works with the teacher in reviewing the plans and discussing the learning objectives, strategies, and instructional activities in the lesson. At its best, the pre-observation conference is a teaching/learning process of shared inquiry with the supervisor acting as a mentor and guide.

Section 3: Lesson Description. This section should accurately reflect the lesson in sufficient detail so that it summarizes the sequence of teacher and student behaviors that occurred. Using chronological order, here you describe the opening of the lesson, how the learning activities developed, the pivotal and important questions that were posed, the media that were used, the actions of the teacher and students, and so on. Include a descriptive summary of all the essential elements of the lesson. This section should be a straight, objective description of what occurred. Here you would want to avoid any subjectivity or making any value judgments, including the use of terms that imply judgments or analysis of the lesson or teacher performance. Two sample lesson descriptions follow:

> At the sound of the bell to begin class all students were in the room. You directed the attention of your students to the "Do Now" that was written on the front sideboard. The full lesson agenda was as follows:
>
> English 10R
>
> Aim: What changes to your rough draft did you make after the conference?
> Do Now: Recall the search you made in yesterday's "Do Now." What events in your past and present are leading you toward your goal?
> Homework: Read to Chapter 18 for Monday. Recall questions and answers from each chapter (total = 12).
>
> You then gave the class 5-10 minutes to complete the "Do Now" writing activity. After the elapsed time you called upon several students to share their responses. Several did. Following this, you then related the "Do Now" to one of the central themes of the novel, *The Catcher in the Rye:* Holden's search for direction and meaning in his life. You then asked students to take out the essays on the novel they had been working on. Volunteers were called upon and they gave three examples from the text that support their theses. One student's thesis stated that Holden was in search of "companionship," while another indicated that Holden was really in search of his dead brother, Allie. Discussion ensued with students defending their theses with examples from the text.
>
> After this discussion, you directed students to work quietly on their rough drafts. You then reminded them of the use of the conference center in the front of the room as you circulated around the room offering suggestions and conferring with individual students on their writing. With 5 minutes left in the period you began the lesson summary by directing students to stop writing and answer the aim question of the day that had been written on

the blackboard. Several students volunteered responses describing the changes they had made in their rough drafts during today's lesson.

As students walked in the door, they picked up a ditto from the front desk. The ditto had the lesson's aim, "How do we divide a monomial by a monomial?" on it along with three "Do Now" questions about determining the perimeter of rectangles and squares and the questions about dividing monomials that you were going to use in the day's lesson. When the bell rang the students were directed to start the "Do Now" problems. You told the class that you would read last night's homework answers to them. As you read the answers, the students checked their homework. A student collected the folders from each row while some students continued to work on the "Do Now" problems. You then asked for volunteers to put the "Do Now" problems on the board. While they did so, you told the other students to hurry up putting their homework in their folders and told Janet, the student who was collecting folders to hurry up and sit down. For the first "Do Now" question, you asked Marlon to explain why he chose answer #3 for the first problem. You asked, "How come it's the circumference and not perimeter?" Alex explained that perimeter is used for rectangles. You asked a second student to explain the difference between a rational and irrational number. You asked if there were any questions about #3.

At 11:05 you directed your students to the development part of the worksheet. You asked, "What do we do to divide monomials?" You wrote the following problem on the overhead: **$30m^4$ divided by 10m.**

You asked, "How do we divide this problem?" You called on Jamal, who explained how to divide monomials. He replied correctly. You then reviewed with them how to do an exponent of power. As students began work on the practice problems, most students needed calculators, which you provided. You reminded students that when they use calculators to reduce a fraction, they could use the ABC key. You circulated around the room as students worked on the problems. At 11:31 you asked the students to look at the summary section of the ditto. You asked students if the answers were true or false. The bell rang to end the period as this review took place.

Notice the use of second person in both lesson descriptions. Its use provides a more personalized, less formal approach to the observation process. Both lesson descriptions are quite expansive and attempt to capture in some detail exactly what occurred and what was said in the classroom by frequent use of paraphrase and direct quotation of key questions.

Section 4: Post-Observation Conference. This section of the report briefly describes what was discussed with the teacher at the post-observation conference meeting. Record details here of discussions of essential elements of the lesson and any information or circumstances that impact the nature or context of the lesson. The section need not be longer than a single short paragraph. Two samples follow:

> At the post-observation meeting for this lesson, you and I met to discuss the observed lesson. You felt that you had achieved your instructional aim in this lesson and that students explored both in their writing and in discussion the ethical choices presented by the use of technology (see lesson plan attached). You felt that all students were actively engaged in the discussion and the journal writing activities. We then discussed the quality of the student responses, particularly their relating the ethical and technology issues to previous literature read in class. You explained that this lesson was an introduction to your students' reading Aldous Huxley's *Brave New World*. We then discussed the commendations and recommendations listed below.

> We met in the mathematics office the next day to discuss the lesson. You recognized that there were problems with how the lesson developed, particularly with the number of distractions and diffi- culty some students had of settling down to work. You did feel, however, that you had achieved the lesson's instructional aim, how to divide a monomial by a monomial. You explained that this was the second day students were working on this topic. You said that the previous day you had developed the rule for division of expo- nents by using a pattern. We then discussed your previous lessons and the observation process itself. We then went on to discus this lesson at length including the following commendations and recommendations.

You will notice that both of the above examples provide context for the observation, giving the teacher the opportunity to explain the circum- stances surrounding the observation itself. In the first example, the teacher explains that the highly philosophical discussion on the ethical uses of technology was an introductory activity to their reading of the satiric novel, *Brave New World*. Similarly, in the second example the teacher explains that the observed lesson was the second in a two-part lesson on monomials. The post-observation summary also points the way to the next two sections of the Supportive Supervision observation model, the commendations and recommendations.

Section 5: Commendations. This section and the ones that follow begin the analysis portion of the report. In the Commendations section of the report you list all of the good points or items that went well in the lesson. You cite evidence of effective practices in the lesson and explain why they were effective. It is also good practice to reference research as often as possible to support your commendations. Two samples follow:

> Good teaching begins with sound and meticulous planning. This lesson shows evidence of outstanding preparation. All the essential elements of an excellent lesson were included: an immediate opening, a meaningful "Do Now" related to the lesson aim, motivation, clearly articulated aims and objectives, varied learning activities, medial summary, directed application, effective questioning, summary, and homework. Your "Do Now" writing exercise was particularly effective. Your students fully participated in the writing because the Ahern quotation was a good choice. It is an intriguing, open-ended observation, and yet served as a good introduction to *Brave New World*. In addition, your directions to use the quotation as a "critical lens" further in the lesson, was in keeping with the new state performance tasks of writing the literary essay. Your choice of Billy Joel's 'Honesty' to play during the "Do Now" exercise could not have been more appropriate.

> Creating a positive classroom atmosphere promotes student achievement. Included in your classroom are several items that make it a warm, welcoming environment. Posters and signs around the room provide positive messages, such as "Top Notch Achievement" and "Reading Is Succeeding." Student work is visible on the bulletin boards, and there is a poster displaying the essential questions that are shared with the social studies class. The room has an overall clean and bright appearance. In addition, students are met with an immediate smile and welcoming attitude when they arrive. When students feel comfortable in their environment, and know their teacher cares them for, they are more willing to participate in activities that require them to stretch and possibly make mistakes. The atmosphere that you have created in this classroom engenders the kind of spirit you see in your students, leading them to certain success.

Notice that aside from citing evidence about a good feature of the lesson, both examples attempt to teach best practice, or why a certain practice or procedure or aspect of the lesson was effective. The first highlights the importance of sound planning and meaningful "Do Now" activities in creating successful lessons, while the second shows how creating a positive classroom environment is an effective practice in promoting student learning.

Section 6: Recommendations. In this section, which follows the commendations, you will list the recommendations. It is not enough to simply point out poor practice or what was not effective in the lesson. It is important to cite evidence gathered during the lesson, documenting the lesson deficiency, and explain why the practice or activity was ineffective. You should also explain how to rectify the poor practice, as well.

As indicated previously, it is best to limit the recommendations to one or two items. A teacher can work on only one or two things at a time. A long list of "faults" in an observed lesson is often counterproductive. It is dispiriting for the teacher and can be overwhelming. It is also important to recognize that there is a graded pattern, or hierarchy of skills, in planning and teaching a lesson. In effect, some teaching skills are far more basic than others. For example, asking a teacher to work on questioning technique, a sophisticated communication skill, makes little sense if the teacher does not know the basics of how to create an instructional aim. Two samples of recommendations follow:

> Effective learning can take place only in a purposeful, orderly environment free of loud noise and off-task behavior. During the lesson there were many times when students were not engaged in an activity. This was evident during the first five minutes of class, immediately following the "Do Now" writing assignment, and during the oral readings. As a result, there was too much inappropriate talking and off task behavior. Your attempt to ignore and "shout over" the talk is an ineffective way to deal with this. It only invites more cross talk and sends the message that you as a teacher will permit a certain level of "noise" while teaching. It is best to stop teaching and tell students why the class cannot continue. Regroup and begin again. Research also shows that the use of external rewards (pizza party for good behavior, etc.) has only limited success in promoting positive behavior in the class. Negative consequences (detention, zeros) have even less success in creating the right environment. What works are well-structured, carefully planned, engaging lessons where all students are actively participating in their own learning. Concentrate your efforts on developing tightly structured, dynamic, fast paced, and engaging lessons, and classroom management problems will cease to be an issue.

You need to develop a more positive rapport with your students. You rarely smiled and did not provide enough positive reinforcement and encouragement to your students during the questioning and instructional activities. To become effective learners willing to take chances and participate, students need to be nurtured and verbally rewarded by their teacher. This is an important part of the teacher-student dynamic that is essential to good teaching. In previous observations this recommendation was made, yet your efforts to improve as evidenced by today's lesson are inconsistent. The observation process is designed to help you learn to critique your own lessons, and every effort must be made to address the recommendations that are made in your classroom observations.

Both examples do more than merely point out the lesson deficiency; each explains why it is poor practice and recommends positive changes. In the first sample, evidence of poor student behavior is given, the reason why this poor behavior occurred is identified, and the supervisor explains why the teacher's efforts to control this is ineffective. She then references research on the subject and suggests an alternative (creating more engaging lessons) to solve the problem. The second sample does something similar. It identifies the teacher's poor rapport with students as a lesson deficiency, explains why developing positive relationships with students is important in the learning process, and urges the teacher to change behavior. The sample also references previous observations, an excellent technique to reinforce to the teacher the need to learn from previous experience, make positive changes, and grow professionally.

Section 7: Summary. The summary ties everything together with a general statement about the teacher's performance and makes an explicit rating of the lesson. In the Supportive Supervision program we suggest using a five-point rating scale—excellent, very good, good, satisfactory, and unsatisfactory. The summary section of the observation can also be used to direct the teacher to take a course of action. Two sample lesson summaries follow:

This was rated as a very good lesson. It is clear that you put a great deal of care into preparing this lesson on immigration. The lesson had a clear focus and a sustained discussion surrounding the main idea. With your mastery over the curriculum I suggest that you help share your lesson ideas with the new member of the eighth-grade team.

This was a satisfactory lesson. You must become a leader in the classroom and keep the lesson on track so that you meet your learning objectives. You must also transform your classroom into an environment conducive to learning. Please take the opportunity to observe Mr. Milazzo and Ms. Merrick, focusing on the ways they interact positively with children during a lesson.

Notice that in both samples the lesson rating is explicitly stated, and the observation summary serves as a springboard or prompt for the teacher to take further action. This can take many forms, including applying what was learned, extending knowledge or skills, observing colleagues, or sharing expertise with others. Thus the observation process can serve as a stimulus for the teacher's own staff development.

A COMPLETE EXAMPLE
OF AN OBSERVATION REPORT

An example of a complete observation report showing how all the various parts of the document fit together follows. The observation report of this middle school lesson on *Tom Sawyer* is rated "very good."

SUPPORTIVE SUPERVISION
CLASSROOM OBSERVATION REPORT

Teacher's Name John Goldman School Central PER 3 10:03 to 10:51

Department English Grade/Course English 7 Level R

Class Register 30 Attendance 27 Observer Ms. Supervisor

Dates: Pre-Observation Conference 12/1/03 Tenure Nontenure_X_

    Observation 12/2/03

    Post-Observation Conference 12/3/03

    Date Report forwarded 12/6/03

Pre-Observation Conference

During the pre-observation conference, you and I discussed the instructional aims in the lesson to be observed. Referring to the lesson plan you had prepared for this meeting, you indicated that the primary aim of the lesson was to have your students understand the internal and external conflicts Tom encounters in the novel *Tom Sawyer*. To accomplish the review, you planned to have students write in their journals and complete a worksheet. We then discussed how using the overhead projector can create a sound instructional focus for a lesson. We then discussed how best to use a pairing group activity both to complete the worksheet review and as a lead-in to the literary paragraph review.

Summary of Lesson Observed

Students entered the room quietly before the bell rang to begin the period, and you instructed them to begin the "Do Now" writing activity. On the overhead projector was written the following:

Aim:	What conflicts have occurred in *The Adventures of Tom Sawyer* up to Chapter 9?
Do Now:	Name and describe one conflict any character faced in one short story we have read this year.
Homework:	Test on chapters

The students worked quietly, writing a response to the "Do Now," as you took attendance. After a few minutes had elapsed, you asked the class to respond to the question regarding conflict. Several students responded and a brief discussion ensued about conflict. You then read the aim of the day's lesson to the class and distributed a worksheet on conflicts in the Twain novel (see attached). This worksheet was projected on the overhead, and students were called upon to complete details about the internal and external conflicts that Tom encounters through the course of the narrative. You then placed the correct responses on the overhead and students copied these notes onto their hard copy of the worksheet.

You then modeled the conflicts developed in Chapter 1 on the overhead. When this was completed, you directed students to work in pairs on completing the other four items on the worksheet. All students complied. As students worked on completing this task, you walked around the room monitoring student work and responding to questions.

With ten minutes remaining in the period, you asked students to get back into rows. You then reviewed the types of conflict and the evidence students found to support the conflict in each of the remaining chapters listed on the worksheet. For the last instructional activity in the lesson, you reviewed the parts of the literature paragraph via the overhead projector. You then instructed students to write an eight-sentence literature paragraph based upon three conflicts that occur in *The Adventures of Tom Sawyer* for homework.

Post-Observation Conference

At the post-observation conference, you and I discussed the lesson and its instructional design and focus. You indicated that the aim of the lesson was to have your students review the major conflicts in the novel *The Adventures of Tom Sawyer* as preparation for their writing a literature paragraph. You felt that you had achieved your instructional aim and that through the discussion, pairing, and responses to questions, students had demonstrated a thorough understanding of the conflicts in the portion of the novel read so far. You felt that they would have little difficulty in doing a good job writing the literature paragraph, which, you explained, was a major outcome of the lesson. We then discussed the commendations and recommendations listed below.

Commendations

- Good organization and tight lesson structure facilitate maximum learning on the part of students. You were able to maximize student learning by creating a well-prepared, meaningful lesson with tight instructional design and structure. All the essential elements of an effective lesson were evident: a meaningful "Do Now" activity linked to the instructional aim, a clearly articulated lesson objective, apperception to prior knowledge, varied student-centered activities, conferencing, appropriate pacing, a summary, and a directed homework activity, again linked to the instructional aim. Particularly effective was the expert use of the overhead projector to develop the learning activities at each stage of the lesson.
- Providing active student learning opportunities results in student success. There was a good variety of active student instructional activities in this lesson. Students wrote quietly on their "Do Nows," responded verbally to your questions, took notes from an overhead projector, worked in pairs completing a worksheet, read from the novel to find textual evidence, and participated in large group discussions. In each learning activity, students were active learners fully engaged in their own learning. Students remained engaged and on task throughout the entire period. To each question raised in class,

many students volunteered responses. You walked around the room during the paired group activity to monitor student work and respond to questions. I observed no off-task or inappropriate behavior by any of your students throughout the lesson.

- Students respond favorably to a friendly, supportive, and positive classroom environment. You have developed an excellent rapport with these seventh-grade students. It is so obvious that they like and respect you as a caring teacher. Your students were eager to participate in all the oral and written learning activities. They were enthusiastic in answering questions posed to them, and were not hesitant in sharing their writing with their classmates. Your excellent interactions with students and the obvious caring and respect that you show toward them were evident throughout the lesson.

- Good questioning technique is an essential key to effective teaching. Your questioning technique in this lesson was quite good, and you used many elements of a Socratic approach to instruction. You asked a variety of questions, one question at a time, and called upon both volunteers and non-volunteers alike to respond. You called on students by name and gave supportive feedback in reacting to their verbal responses. You posed many higher order thinking questions such as "Explain why the internal conflict Tom experiences is more difficult to resolve than his problems with Sid," and maintained sufficient wait time to allow students time to think. You did not repeat student responses, nor respond to call-outs, and requested that students speak up so that other students could hear what was said.

Recommendations

- The ability to share information cooperatively in groups is an essential skill that all students must master. In this lesson, there were seven pairs, seven singles, one triple, and one quadruple group arrangement. It is not good practice to allow students to opt out of group work. When getting students to form groups, it is best to direct students rather than ask them to do so. By asking rather than directing students to form pairs, some students will decide not to do so and will opt to work alone or in different numbered arrangements. Formulate your grouping prior to class and include this in your lesson plan.

Summary

This was a very good lesson. You exhibit all the personal qualities and teaching skills necessary for mastering the art and science of teaching. Please take advantage of professional workshops in order to learn and experiment with new techniques. You may also wish to visit other members of the seventh-grade team to discover how they integrate group strategies in their lessons.

OBSERVER_____

Date:_____

TEACHER_____

Date:_____

THE TEACHER'S SIGNATURE DOES NOT SIGNIFY AGREEMENT WITH THE STATEMENTS IN THIS REPORT. THE TEACHER HAS THE RIGHT TO FILE A WRITTEN RESPONSE THAT WILL BE PART OF THE TEACHER'S FILE.

The ORIGINAL copy of this report is to be given to the teacher. Additional copies are to be filed with the (a) Dept. Chairperson, (b) District Coordinator, (c) Building Principal, and (d) District Personnel Office.

THE SUPPORTIVE SUPERVISION OBSERVATION REPORT

Using the Supportive Supervision structured essay format for your classroom observations will not only improve the quality of your observations, but it will provide invaluable feedback for the teacher. It will provide meaningful and rich detail on the quality of the teacher's instructional skills and methodology. Its use will signal to the teacher the paramount importance of instructional delivery, the necessity to grow and improve skills, and that what occurs in the classroom is the very heart of school.

Figure 6.3   Supportive Supervision Classroom Observation Report (Form)

Teacher's Name _____   School _____   Period _____

Time _____

Department _____   Grade/Course _____   Level _____

Class Register _____   Attendance _____   Observer _____

This report is to be used by the Supervisor to report:
  (a) Details of all observation/conferences held
  (b) Details of classroom activities observed, and
  (c) The supervisor's analysis and recommendations.

It is to be signed and dated by both the teacher and the observer. The teacher may attach comments that will become part of the official file.

Dates: Pre-Observation Conference   _____   Tenure ____   Non-Tenure ____
          Observation   _____
          Post-Observation Conference _____
          Date Report Forwarded   _____

- -

Pre-Observation Conference

Summary of Lesson Observed

Post-Observation Discussion

Commendations

Recommendations

Summary

OBSERVER _____   Date:_____

TEACHER _____   Date:_____

THE TEACHER'S SIGNATURE DOES NOT SIGNIFY AGREEMENT WITH THE STATE-MENTS IN THIS REPORT. THE TEACHER HAS THE RIGHT TO FILE A WRITTEN RESPONSE THAT WILL BE PART OF THE TEACHER'S FILE.

The ORIGINAL copy of this report is to be given to the teacher. Additional copies are to be filed with the (a) Dept. Chairperson, (b) District Coordinator, (c) Building Principal, and (d) District Personnel Office.

Professional Development

Professional Development (PD) is the fourth component in the Supportive Supervisory program and appears at the bottom of the page following Observation in the continuum. Although a general outline of the year's PD program can be drawn up when establishing goals at the beginning of the year, its placement after Observation suggests that PD should also be based upon the observed needs of the teacher. Taking a broad view of what constitutes PD activities, in this chapter we explain how to be proactive in providing PD opportunities to your staff and how to tie PD programs to instructional goals. We also describe different kinds of individual and group PD activities with representative examples. Finally, we provide a template for outside conference reports.

PD FOR ALL STAFF

Professional Development is not a one-shot deal. It is neither a reward for good service, a treat for your good teachers, nor a break from the everyday routine of school. We believe that effective, well-conceived PD must be the primary mechanism for the continuation of instructional development and, eventually, increased student achievement. The opportunities that you create for the professional development needs of your staff are a significant part of your efforts to create a great school. PD is not just for your new staff members; veteran teachers and support personnel alike will benefit from strong PD programs. Despite the number of years of teaching experience they may have, all of your teachers can grow professionally and learn how to incorporate best practice in their classrooms.

Although teaching has always been a challenging task, it is becoming more so as we struggle to meet the complex social and educational needs of young people in the 21st century. The most recent federal educational initiative, the No Child Left Behind legislation, demands greater school and teacher accountability for student achievement.[48] Today's teachers constantly need to upgrade skills and develop new teaching strategies. Teachers need to learn and master the newest and best ways to teach children in the fast-paced, dynamic American culture, with its shifting social and family values, economic uncertainty, increased mobility, and changing demographics. Teaching is both an exquisite art and a complex science that requires a lifetime of study, observation, and practice to master.

PLANNING AND FLEXIBILITY

In the Supportive Supervision program, good professional development programs do not take place independently from other components of school supervision, but are part of the process, fully integrated with the others. Given the necessary resources, the programs you put in place depend not only on the district, school, staff, and departmental goals that were established early in the school year, but also on the teacher feedback you receive, the classroom observations that you have conducted, the meetings you have had with your administrative staff, and the analyses you have made of other factors in the school. In our program, PD is both a planned and a flexible response to teacher and program needs. It is planned in that a comprehensive, ongoing focus or plan should be in place early in the school year, yet there should be flexibility, room, and resources available to respond to immediate needs.

A specific illustration will make this last point clearer. Suppose that in response to a new district student placement policy and changes in state law, you plan to present a yearlong series of afterschool workshops to help your staff deal with issues of inclusion. In lieu of traditional separate department meetings for the current school year, you plan to have your staff gather as a whole group and participate in a variety of afterschool workshops dealing with this important change. You arrange for curriculum specialists, district personnel, and outside speakers to lead workshops where your staff will discuss the changes in policy and law, design model lessons, learn new methodology to differentiate instruction, share teaching experiences, and practice effective classroom management techniques. However, as the first quarter grades are analyzed with the administrative team in late October, you identify a very serious lack of student achievement in mathematics. Is it better to continue with the planned program of PD on inclusion with members of the math department, or would it be wiser to exempt them from this and respond to this immediate need? We would argue the latter. In our view it would be more effective to be flexible and redirect PD resources for your math teachers toward content specific workshops in best practice in teaching math and other activities related to student achievement.

A BROAD VIEW OF PD

In the Supportive Supervision program we take a broad view of what constitutes PD, to include many activities beyond attendance at outside conferences and commercial workshops. As was alluded to in Chapter 1, traditional professional development (off-site, all-day conferences and workshops) has its place and can be quite rewarding, but we incorporate into our repertoire other, less expensive ways to help teachers grow professionally. Sending large numbers of teachers out for training or to attend workshops can disrupt the continuity of classroom instruction, and it is often difficult, if not impossible, to find competent substitutes. Rather than looking outside, we have found that it is often better to look within.

In the Supportive Supervision program, PD may include a variety of in-house professional activities, from having small groups of teachers collaborate on writing lesson plans to conducting grade-level discussion groups. These activities may also include regular planning sessions with beginning teachers, peer observations of master teachers, faculty presentations, the assignment and mentoring of student teachers, instructional workshops at department meetings, the writing of curriculum guides, collaborating on writing grants, interdisciplinary projects, writing new program proposals, grade-level meetings, leading focus group discussions, providing opportunities for teachers for reflection, the reading of professional literature, video presentations, teleconferencing, and the use of technology.

Some PD Activities in the Supportive Supervision Program

➤ Peer observations
➤ Demonstration lessons
➤ Before- and afterschool workshops
➤ Small group lesson planning
➤ Observing master teachers
➤ Making faculty and departmental presentations
➤ Mentoring beginning and student teachers
➤ Creating new curriculum
➤ Collaborating on grant incentives
➤ Participating in interdisciplinary projects
➤ Writing new program proposals
➤ Participating in grade level meetings
➤ Leading focus group discussions
➤ Providing reflective opportunities
➤ Developing teaching portfolios
➤ Reading professional literature
➤ Keeping a teaching journal
➤ Viewing programs on video or DVD
➤ Creating video presentations
➤ Videotaping lessons
➤ Video and teleconferencing

USE A VARIETY OF PD ACTIVITIES

All of the PD activities in our Supportive Supervision program can help new and existing staff members gain new knowledge and skills, create new curriculum and methods, adapt and improve teaching methodology, and grow professionally. Some of these PD activities are more suitable than others for the beginning teacher, the experienced teacher, and the marginal teacher. For example, all three types of teachers will benefit from the regular reading of professional literature, yet beginning teachers will benefit most by assembling a teaching portfolio. Similarly, it makes little sense to place a beginning teacher on a committee to write new curriculum, which would be better served by a more experienced teacher.

Workshops

Conducting before- and afterschool workshops is an excellent way to engage all staff members in productive staff development activities. It is cost-effective, can be adapted to a variety of purposes and formats, and most important, it does not disrupt regular classroom instruction. Topics can be identified through the observation process, a faculty committee to develop the agenda, or a needs-assessment survey. The most successful workshops are those that have broad appeal and application, but are sharply targeted on a single focus area or theme: reading strategies for content area teachers, motivating the reluctant learner, recognizing at-risk students, using different learning modalities, and so on.

Group Planning

Providing time and space for a small number of teachers to collaborate on group lesson planning and participate in grade-level meetings can be very effective in promoting professional development. These activities work best for staff members teaching the same course or grade-level teams teaching the same students. Placing beginning teachers in the group is a good strategy, for they can gain much from the expertise of their more experienced colleagues. To facilitate full participation, try to limit the number of teachers to no more than four or five per group. As with all ad hoc groups or committees, to keep the group on task and working smoothly, it is best to provide a very specific charge and a timeline to complete it.

Observing

Observing a master teacher can be a powerful professional development activity. Effective for all categories of teachers, observing master teachers, or perhaps teachers with a specific strength, can do much to help teachers improve the quality of classroom instruction and teaching skills. However, it is not enough to have teachers merely observe. It is crucial that the observing teachers process and internalize what has been observed. This should be a major focus of the observation itself. To have them gain the most from this experience, have the observing teachers write about what was observed and meet with you to review the strengths of the lesson in a nonevaluative manner. As a Supportive Supervisor you should support and stimulate this reflective process and help your teachers incorporate what was learned into their own teaching.

We recommend that you have the observing teacher observe with a purpose. For example, you will recall that in Chapter 6, Mr. Bates's lesson lacked good class participation because of poor questioning technique. To help Mr. Bates improve, it would be helpful to ask him to observe his colleague Mrs. Lewis, noting the kinds of questions she asks and how she uses them to generate student participation. After the observation, meet with Mr. Bates to review his observation. He should discuss the lesson with Mrs. Lewis, as well. Of course, the master teacher's voluntary cooperation in being observed is essential. We have found that most outstanding teachers appreciate the recognition they receive as "master" teachers, and are more than happy to share their expertise with others. In many ways your master teachers are one of your most important tools for providing professional development for your staff.

Faculty Presentations

Having staff members collaborate in making faculty presentations is another excellent professional development technique. Effective teachers and those who have acquired a particular expertise are the ones most likely to benefit from this activity. For example, you might ask your English as a Second Language specialists to prepare a presentation to the entire faculty about the new immersion program for students with limited English skills and how regular classroom teachers can best help these students succeed. If successful, this faculty presentation will have a dual benefit. The faculty who attend will be better informed about how best to teach ESL students, while the ESL staff members who put the program together will have clarified their goals and student expectations, and have done significant research and reflection on best practice in their field. In addition, these teachers become resources for the entire faculty. A variety of formats can be used for faculty presentations. A panel of experts, a PowerPoint presentation, large and small group discussion, video segments or demonstrations, a question and answer session, or any combination of these can all be used effectively. However, similar to a good lesson, those presentations that work best are those that are engaging and involve the participants in a variety of hands-on instructional activities.

Department Presentations

Department presentations are naturally more limited in scope, yet these can be extremely effective in showcasing teacher expertise. To encourage a spirit of sharing and collaboration among teachers in a department, it helps to dedicate a portion of each department meeting to staff presentations. These can be as simple as sharing model lesson plans, giving brief oral reports on workshops and meetings, or distributing handouts collected at conferences. Teachers can be asked to do mini lessons on various aspects of their teaching or the course curriculum, or to participate in more elaborate collaborative efforts among several department members. Interdisciplinary meetings of two or more related departments (English and social studies, science and mathematics, art and music) can also provide successful PD opportunities.

Interdisciplinary Projects

Interdisciplinary project committees can be effective PD tools as well. Curriculum connections across disciplines and the sharing of instructional approaches can be beneficial and effect positive academic results. While recent research supports an interdisciplinary approach to classroom instruction to improve academic achievement,[49] less attention has been given to the benefits teachers receive from close interaction and planning with colleagues across discipline areas. Interdisciplinary committees are powerful vehicles of professional development. Participants report gaining new content knowledge, fresh approaches to instructional delivery, and improved teaching skills.

Mentoring

As was noted before, it is an excellent idea to develop a close working relationship with local colleges and universities that offer degrees in undergraduate and graduate education. Mentoring student teachers can be a deeply rewarding experience and an exceptional PD opportunity for many of your teachers. This is particularly true of your good teachers, who if paired with student teachers are often inspired and motivated to achieve classroom excellence. A key feature of all teacher education programs, student teaching can be a valuable tool in your school's total professional development program. Accepting and placing student teachers in your school, as well as welcoming student observers, not only provides instructional opportunities for those learning to be teachers, but it also can function as a wonderful catalyst to help revitalize a veteran staff. Mentor teachers can gain as much as student teachers in the teacher-learner process. The energy and idealism of youth can be a powerful and galvanizing force spurring mentors to excel at their craft. The regular presence of student teachers in your school will often enrich the professional interactions and conversations among your staff members, as well. It should also be noted that welcoming large numbers of student teachers into your faculty will provide you with a rich pool of potential teaching candidates in the hiring process.

We also strongly endorse a mentoring program for beginning teachers. As was discussed earlier, studies show that a mentoring and teacher induction program will do much to develop and retain good teachers. Well-matched mentors, and providing opportunities for close collaboration on curriculum, lesson planning, and peer observation are important elements in ensuring a successful mentoring program. As with the positive benefits and synergy that so often results between the mentor and student teacher, the same is true with beginning teachers. Both gain in the mentoring process.

Writing Projects

Most often thought of as a purely instructional activity, curriculum development can function as a worthwhile avenue of professional development, as well. Usually, teachers who are writing new curriculum do not work in isolation. Rather, small teams of teachers are given the time and resources to work together in committee to produce instructional documents that can be used by other teachers. Ideally, the resulting teacher guides, curriculum materials, instructional units, and lesson plans are geared to the particular needs of the students in the school, the community, or the district. In addition to the benefits received by the teachers, the curriculum writers themselves gain immeasurably in this collaborative process by researching and sharing new ideas, adapting existing concepts and strategies to new material, and producing new instructional materials.

Collaborating on writing grant applications and new program proposals are two excellent opportunities for the professional development of your staff. Working together, teachers can complete program requests or grant applications to apply for funding or approval for a new program. New program applications and funding grants vary widely. They can be a small, purely local, district or school initiative, or a large regional, state, or national program. Often these applications are multi-part documents that require applicants to do research, write essays explaining the purpose and goals of the project, budget materials and supplies, and provide appropriate documentation of need. You should encourage teachers to collaborate and apply for program and funding grants. In addition to the resources gained, winning a grant or program approval can have a very positive effect in boosting teacher morale and professionalism. Beyond this are the added PD benefits of teacher collaboration and the sharing of ideas.

Leading Groups

Encouraging teachers on your staff to lead a focus group discussion is another way you can provide valuable professional development opportunities. In the Supportive Supervision program, administrators need to be proactive and seek out such leadership opportunities for their staff. Often you will learn of these discussion groups and opportunities first. Consider who on your staff would be best suited to lead that afterschool discussion with parents or community members, or who would be best able to lead a small group discussion during a faculty program or departmental meeting. We have found that teachers who take responsibility for leading group discussions, whatever the subject, gain confidence and self-assurance in their own efficacy as teaching professionals and in their ability to listen and respond to others appropriately. In general, discussion leaders improve their own social, interpersonal, and leadership skills, which are valuable assets in the classroom.

Reflective Opportunities

In the Supportive Supervision program you should provide a variety of reflective opportunities for your staff so that they can grow as teaching professionals. In addition to the reflective opportunities built into the formal observation process discussed earlier,[50] you should encourage your staff to become thoughtful and reflective practitioners. One of the very best ways to do this is through the use of a teaching journal. All teachers on your staff should be encouraged to reflect in writing on what they do. This can take the form of simple notations written at the end of the day on what worked and what did not work in the classroom. These comments can be collected in a separate journal or notebook or kept with the lesson plan book itself. A teaching journal can also take a broader form and become a repository of the teacher's daily musings and thoughts about the teaching process itself, the curriculum, the school environment, and working with students. Although research supports its use as a way to help both marginal and beginning teachers improve,[51] all teachers can certainly benefit from this reflective practice.

Another way you can encourage reflective practice among your staff is by encouraging them to keep a teaching portfolio. A central feature of the rigorous National Board for Professional Teaching Standards certification process,[52] teaching portfolios are most often kept by student teachers and teachers seeking a voluntary national certification. As with all portfolios, the selection and collection process of what items and samples of work to include in the portfolio is a powerful reflective practice and an effective teaching methodology. Seeking national certification and assembling a portfolio can be a good strategy in motivating veteran "good" teachers to strive for excellence. In some states probationary teachers seeking permanent certification must submit along with the written application a teaching skills video showcasing the teacher's use of best practice in the classroom.[53]

Professional Literature

Encouraging your staff to read professional literature is an important element in creating a positive professional environment in your school. We have learned that to get staff members to read professional journals and literature regularly, we must do more than just place journals in a magazine rack on the wall in the hopes that someone will read them. As we have indicated before, one of your responsibilities as a "teacher of teachers" is to keep current and know the latest research and best practice in the field. Both time and money are well spent in subscribing to and reading educational magazines and professional journals. Distributing copies of articles and pertinent pieces to targeted members of your staff is an excellent technique to spur interest in a subject and initiate a professional conversation. Although posting relevant articles from journals or items clipped from newspapers dealing with education issues on a bulletin board has some merit, it is not as effective as targeting and routing a piece to a particular person. Using the Bates example once again, as you identify good articles on questioning skills you would forward them to him, perhaps with a handwritten note attached. Finally, some schools have had some success using prepackaged PD booklets. Available from several commercial publishers and professional organizations, these programs consist of booklets and easy-to-read brochures on teaching best practice and current research and issues in education. Designed to be routed or placed in the teacher's mailbox on a regular basis, these informative, upbeat booklets are usually well received.

Technology

Technology can be a valuable ally in your campaign to provide quality PD opportunities for your staff. There are many commercially produced professional development programs on video or DVD. Comprehensive in the range of subjects and topics available, these video/DVD programs are often quite expensive, and they can vary widely in quality. As with textbook purchases, it's best to request a free trial period from the publisher and have a small team of teachers, counselors, media specialists, and/or administrators preview the videos or DVDs to evaluate a program's quality and suitability for your needs.

Making video presentations, videotaping lessons, and participating in video- and teleconferencing can be rewarding professional development activities for your staff, as well. Video can be a very effective PD tool. A powerful way to help a teacher improve instruction is to have the teacher videotape his own lesson and then critique it. Let's use Mr. Bates as a model again; a very effective way to improve his teaching would be to videotape one of his lessons and have him view the tape focusing on the level of student participation and the quality of his questions. The videotape accurately records the questioning data while Mr. Bates's critique of his performance fosters self-reflection and analysis.

BASE PD ON NEEDS

The most effective PD opportunities are those that match the professional needs of the individual teacher or the goals and objectives of a particular department or program. However exciting they may appear in the promotional letter or brochure, outside conferences and workshops that do not match these needs should be avoided. For example, suppose that after the first month of school, Ms. Templeton, your new science teacher, who is bright and eager to learn, seems to be floundering. She understands the need to include all the essential elements in creating her lessons, yet she has great difficulty doing so. Her uneven performance in the classroom is satisfactory at best. While it certainly would have value for Templeton to attend an upcoming luncheon and workshop on science and girls' education with the astronaut Sally Ride at the local college, it would be a better use of resources and her PD time to perhaps forgo this conference and instead focus her efforts on improving lesson development and creating more positive interactions with students. This may take the form of viewing a video series on planning instruction, planning with teachers in the department, or attending instructional workshops more closely related to her observed need.

Or consider the case of Mr. Kramer, a veteran Spanish teacher, who is having difficulty with the poor behavior of students in his classes. Sending him off to a two-day state conference sponsored by the Foreign Language Teacher Association has little educational value for him in meeting his stated goal of improving classroom management. It would be far better and more cost-effective to have him use professional development time to work on improving organizational skills and the quality of classroom instruction. Among other things, Mr. Kramer could observe colleagues with good classroom management skills, collaborate with other members of the department in writing lessons, or keep a teaching journal monitoring effective classroom behaviors. Mr. Kramer could attend an afterschool workshop in his own school on creating exciting lessons, view a videotape or DVD on classroom management, or perhaps attend a local workshop on Lee Canter's Assertive Discipline.[54]

PD AND ACADEMIC ACHIEVEMENT

While many of the professional development opportunities you provide for your staff will be based on the observed instructional needs of your teachers, as in the case of Mr. Kramer and Ms. Templeton, other opportunities should be directly tied to student achievement. PD goals and objectives for the school as a whole and individual departments or grade levels are often best set after looking closely at all the cumulative student achievement data at the end of the school year.

The following scenario will make this point clearer. Suppose that last March all of your eighth-grade students took a new state writing exam. You receive the test results in June and they are not good. It appears that too few students (less than 10%) scored in the highest achievement category on the exam. The state norm in the top grouping is 22%. These achievement data become the prompt for the professional development you will provide next year. You would certainly want to develop a comprehensive instructional improvement plan to elevate the writing achievement of not only your top students, but also of all of your students in the school. The existing writing program and training manuals might be revised over the summer, and new goals and objectives might be established. Perhaps all sixth-, seventh-, and eighth-grade English teachers might collaborate on creating new cross-grade writing units. During the upcoming school year this same team of teachers might also receive several hours of PD training by outside writing consultants familiar with the state exam, while additional training in general writing methodology might be provided for all staff. Finally, you might encourage the creation of several interdisciplinary writing units and other writing across the curriculum initiatives in the content areas, as well. All of these PD initiatives are a direct result of your analysis of student achievement data.

FEEDBACK

Teacher feedback is an essential part of the professional development component in the Supportive Supervision program. We believe it is always best practice to debrief teachers soon after they attend conferences or workshops. This debriefing can take several forms. Requesting a presentation at an upcoming department or faculty meeting is a good practice because it not only requires that the attendee reflect upon, articulate, and apply what was learned at the conference, but it extends the knowledge and skills gained there to others. A good solid discussion of the merits and suitability of what was learned at the workshop will often ensue after a teacher makes a presentation on a conference or workshop to colleagues in the school or department. This kind of professional interaction and dialogue is a powerful motivating factor in helping good teachers strive for excellence and should always be encouraged at meetings.

WRITTEN REPORTS

In addition to these oral presentations, teachers who attend outside conferences or training sessions can be asked to complete a written conference report. These conference reports are valuable tools in your PD program. As with making an oral presentation, writing a report can serve as a powerful reflective vehicle. If sufficiently detailed, it can help teachers process the new information and skills acquired at the workshop and consider ways to apply the new knowledge and skills to their own teaching. Written reports underscore the importance you place on professional development to your staff, and they can help you determine whether the workshop is suitable for other members of your staff, as well.

In addition to follow-up written reports, all district- or school-designed PD workshops or training sessions should include built-in evaluation forms or surveys. It is best to structure time for participants to complete these at the end of the program, rather than leave this for teachers to complete later on. Evaluation is a customary feature of all good PD programs, and will provide you with invaluable feedback on what was successful or not successful in the program. With this information you can better make adjustments to the present PD program and in planning for the future.

A FINAL WORD ON PD

Any time teachers interact on a professional level related to identified goals and acquire new knowledge, improve teaching skills, or learn more effective strategies to improve instruction, we are in the realm of professional development. Master teachers were not born with the knowledge of how to achieve excellence in the classroom; they learned it. In fact, great teachers are great learners, always ready to acquire new skills and eager to find new ways to grow professionally. We believe strongly that teaching is both an exquisite art and a complex science that requires a lifetime of study, observation, and practice to master.

Figure 7.1   Outside Conference Report

Name _____ School _____ Report Date _____

Date of Conference _____ Location _____

Title of Conference _____ Presenter _____

Format (Briefly describe how the conference was organized, its length and its method of presentation. Attach an agenda if distributed.)

Summary (Briefly summarize what the conference was about, its stated objectives and information about activities, presentations, topics, or subjects.)

Application (What did you learn from this workshop or conference? What relevance does this new knowledge or skill have to your teaching? How will this new knowledge or skill help you as a teacher?)

Evaluation (How worthwhile was the conference? Did the conference achieve its stated objectives? Did it meet your needs? Would it be suitable for others? Please answer on the back of this sheet and attach samples of handouts.)

Extensive Professional Commitment

The fifth component in the Supportive Supervision program is Extensive Professional Commitment (EPC). In the continuum EPC appears at the bottom left of the page, following Professional Development. Though it appears in this position, developing an EPC in your staff occurs throughout the year. In this chapter we define what we mean by an Extensive Professional Commitment and offer some examples of teachers with EPC contrasted with teachers who lack it. Then we discuss how to build a consensus on core values. We conclude this chapter by examining the five critical components that can establish an EPC environment in the school: modeling EPC behaviors, making a personal appeal for a commitment, promoting a child-centered philosophy, establishing professional dress, and providing extra help.

WHAT IS EPC?

In a very real sense all teachers make a professional commitment when they are hired. In very basic terms the newly hired teacher signs a contract or employment agreement in which the teacher makes a commitment to provide a professional service (instructing students) and the employer agrees to pay a certain amount of compensation (salary, benefits, etc.). Simple enough, but as we discussed earlier, really great schools are staffed with teachers who do much more than that. They provide a level of professional service well above the basic commitment to provide instruction to the children who are in their classes. Great schools contain professionals who extend themselves way beyond the narrow limits of what is required by the contract, or what is expressly stated in the teacher's terms and conditions of employment. These professionals are dedicated and committed to the success of all the children in their school. We call this dedication and willingness to go above and beyond, an extensive professional commitment, or EPC.

Earlier in our discussion of the six components of the Supportive Supervision program, we defined EPC very broadly as the observed behaviors of a teacher's dedication and commitment to the school, its shared values and culture, its philosophy of education, and its students. Much more than just being "professional" in and out of the classroom, EPC teachers share a core value of the primacy of children. They believe that in a school the education and welfare of children are primary, and that all decisions should place the best interests of the child before any other consideration. EPC teachers have a child-centered commitment to be the very best teachers they can be and to do whatever it takes to help every child succeed.

An extensive professional commitment from all staff members is so important that we sincerely doubt that a great school can be built without it.

EPC: EASILY RECOGNIZED, DIFFICULT TO DEFINE

Perhaps the term *extensive professional commitment* will be easier to understand by looking at a few concrete examples. What we mean by EPC can be brought into sharp relief by contrasting teachers who have an extensive professional commitment with those who lack this quality but nonetheless remain "good" teachers.

As portrayed in Figure 8.1, teachers who are good staff members but lack EPC regularly do the right things and perform what is expected of them as professional educators. But teachers with EPC go beyond this expected level of performance and professionalism. They freely give of their time to help kids. Thus, EPC teachers forgo the latest TV reality show to come back to school to attend the evening concert, volunteer to be in the talent show, and sacrifice lunchtime socializing with friends in the cafeteria or teachers' lounge to be in the classroom for their students. Placing the needs of children first, EPC teachers support and nurture the success of every child because they are committed and dedicated individuals.

IS THE EPC TEACHER REALISTIC?

Some may feel that the EPC teacher profile we have presented here is unrealistic. However, from our own experience working with many teachers with an extensive professional commitment over the years, we have found

Figure 8.1   Good Teachers Versus EPC Teachers

A good teacher . . .
Is available after school for extra help or make-ups twice a week for students who request it.

An EPC teacher . . .
Arrives early and stays late because that is when he or she can best help kids who might need some extra attention.

A good teacher . . .
Buys a banner from the booster club for the bulletin board to support the basketball team.

An EPC teacher . . .
Buys a banner and drops by the gym before that evening's game just to say good luck.

A good teacher . . .
Gives alternate assignments to student musicians who miss class because of the concert.

An EPC teacher . . .
Gives alternate assignments, and attends the evening band concert.

A good teacher . . .
Takes lunch with colleagues in the teacher's cafeteria each day but is never late to class afterward.

An EPC teacher . . .
Takes a short lunch to give extra help to students who can meet no other time.

A good teacher . . .
Attends the faculty-student talent show.

An EPC teacher . . .
Has little talent, cannot sing, but volunteers to be in the show anyway.

A good teacher . . .
Served as a class advisor several years ago.

An EPC teacher . . .
Was a class advisor, but now agrees to advise a new alternative music and dance club because the kids asked.

A good teacher . . .
Recognizes academic achievement in class, motivates students to learn, and has a low failure rate.

An EPC teacher . . .
Has all students succeed in class and will not accept or allow a student to fail.

A good teacher . . .
Uses proper procedure for the occasional discipline referral to administration.

An EPC teacher . . .
Has never made a discipline referral.

that not to be the case. Teachers who exhibit EPC behaviors do indeed arrive early, stay late, seem to be always available, and are the first to volunteer for whatever needs to be done in the school. Far from being starry-eyed Pollyannas, EPC teachers are quite realistic about the sometimes overwhelming challenges they face working with students. They know how hard it is to try to reach every child. They know how frustrating it can be to get and keep some students on track. It takes an extensive effort to motivate the unmotivated, and to teach the disaffected, the bored, the at risk, and the ones that seem to lack even the most basic of academic and social skills. Yet they never give up, believing in the intrinsic value and worth of every child. They believe in the values of caring, perseverance, hard work, study, and dedication to task. The teacher with the extensive professional commitment will do whatever it takes to see that each child succeeds.

From what we describe here you may recognize a few EPC teachers in your school. In the really great school, however, every grade level and every department has many teachers who fit this profile. You might ask, "How does this happen and is this possible?" The answer is a resounding "Yes!" Staffing a school with a majority of teachers who exhibit EPC qualities and behaviors is certainly not an impossible task. We believe you can create a climate where EPC can thrive, where EPC teachers are not the exception, but the norm. Doing so is a long-term project, and you should not expect success overnight. As with most things that are important in teaching and education, it begins with the hiring process.

HIRING TEACHERS WITH THE RIGHT STUFF

As stated before, you should seek to hire teachers who have the values, character, personality, and willingness to make an extensive professional commitment to your school. You will recall that in Chapter 3, "Hiring the Right Teachers," we discussed the critical need to hire teachers with the "right stuff," which we defined as teachers who have the character, desire, attitude, personal qualities, and potential to become great teachers. We explained that teachers with the right stuff are those who have a burning desire and enthusiasm for teaching. Within the résumé and especially during the interview process and the demonstration lesson, teachers with the right stuff show evidence of caring attitudes and that they love teaching and working with children. They express a sincere desire to make a positive difference in the lives of students and are willing to work hard at being the best they can be. These are the teachers who place the academic, social, and developmental needs of children first. This is the right stuff in the people you are looking for to staff your school. Out of this right stuff you can begin to shape and guide your beginning teachers to make an extensive professional commitment.

Determining who has the potential right stuff to make an extensive professional commitment is a critical element in the Supportive Supervision hiring process. It is best to deal with the issue of professional commitment head-on at the initial interview. The first time we meet with the candidate we explain EPC and the kind of professional commitment we expect from new teachers, and we look closely at the prospective teacher's response. That response weighs heavily in our decision-making process. We evaluate the candidate's sincerity and look for those who are truly excited about making that commitment to our school. It is here at the interview stage that we can best gauge the applicant's suitability for our school by examining how he or she reacts to our expectations of professional commitment.

An Interview Story

The following story about a recent interview for a new position teaching social studies will make this point clearer. To relax candidates we begin most interviews in pretty much the same way with an "easy" question related to the person's aspirations to become a teacher.

The candidate sat uneasily facing a group of strangers seated around a long table. In response to the question about why he wanted to be a teacher, the candidate took a deep breath and began slowly, but he soon relaxed and warmed to his subject.

> Well, I want to teach because I love history. I've always been interested in history. Ever since I can remember I was fascinated by the past. My interest really began when I was about eight. My dad was a Civil War buff and in the summer he would take the family on visits to Civil War historic sites and battlefields. I remember we went to Shiloh and Gettysburg, Antietam and Manassas, Vicksburg . . . we visited them all. Ever since then, history has been alive for me. I have had a passion for American history and finding out about our past, our roots. You see, history is not a dead subject, but a living treasury and, if read properly, a signpost to the future endeavors of man. . . .

The candidate continued to wax eloquent on his passion for American history and its rich meaning in his life.

His academic credentials were impeccable, and his knowledge of history was quite impressive, but we chose not to hire him for that open social studies position at the middle school. Though he was quite personable and certainly knowledgeable, his response to this opening inquiry and other more direct questions about professional commitment revealed that he really didn't have what we look for in a teacher. More interested in his subject than in teaching children, he didn't have the "right stuff."

The "Right Stuff" and EPC

The teachers you have identified as having the right stuff and have hired will become the ones who are most likely to make an extensive professional commitment at your school. In many ways, the right stuff is the necessary ingredient, or raw material, out of which the beginning teacher makes that commitment. EPC behaviors are much more likely in a teacher whom you hire with this right stuff than one who does not have these qualities. In other words, with a sincere and deep love of teaching children, a passion for subject, and the right personal qualities, the beginning teacher will somehow always be available to help students all the time, will be happy to volunteer to advise that new club, or will never be too busy to attend the evening games and concerts. In short, these special new hires who have the right stuff are the ones who will become your EPC teachers.

As mentioned in our hiring chapter, teachers with the right stuff are the ones who have the greatest potential as teachers. In our experience, beginning teachers with the right stuff exhibit EPC behaviors right away, and many that we hired became great teachers as they worked hard to master the art and science of their craft.

EPC Is a Character Issue

We recognize that making an extensive professional commitment is to a large degree a character and values issue. As such, it will be an easy, natural progression for those who have the personal qualities and character we have described as the right stuff. For others whose character and values are less in accord with this, there will be no natural and easy development to EPC. As these values and character traits are more alien to them, it will be a much more challenging task for them to make that commitment.

While it is a difficult task to get someone who lacks right-stuff qualities when they are hired to make an extensive professional commitment later on when they begin teaching, it is not impossible. As educators we understand full well the difficulty of effecting changes in attitude and behavior. We know that it takes time, perseverance, a supportive climate, and a multipronged approach. We know this is hard work, but changing attitudes and behavior can and does happen. As a supportive supervisor you play the key role in establishing the right environment and in motivating your staff to make that commitment.

Core Values

Change happens slowly, and we believe it begins with the values that sustain the school. It has become increasingly clear that real change and systemic reform are not possible without an agreed-upon set of values and beliefs. Research has demonstrated that shared common values and moral leadership are vitally important in all school reform efforts.[55] In the Supportive Supervision program, supervisors must seek to build a consensus on core values and consistently demonstrate moral leadership in all the actions and decisions that are made.

Identifying these core values invites some reflection. Values, of course, will vary somewhat from place to place, from one school district to another, depending upon many factors. Socioeconomics plays a major part as does the cultural heritage and backgrounds of the families within the school community. For example, one school might place great value on teaching art, music, literature, and the performing arts, while another might place much more emphasis on its athletic program, another on science and technology. A strong belief in competition and a spirit of individual excellence and achievement might inform one school, while another might more highly prize cooperation and teamwork. Such values as competitiveness, teamwork, artistic expression, or athletic prowess are certainly important, but are not at the real core, the very heart of what we value in school.

Supportive Supervision Core Values

First and foremost, honesty and integrity are the bedrock values without which no school or any social, business, or cultural organization can function well. Certainly, freedom, respect for our social institutions, and cultural diversity are fundamental values, as well. Other values are also important: sensitivity to the needs of others, determination, hard work, academic success, friendship, understanding, and compassion.[56] Though one can argue the inclusion of additional values to this list, these core values are the ones most likely to be found in all great schools. Such values not only inform all decisions and actions that are made in a school, but they help to create and sustain a school climate that encourages academic achievement and extraordinary efforts by the professional staff to commit to the success of all children.

Core Values Help Create an EPC Climate

Promulgated by the words you speak and the actions you take as an instructional and moral leader of the school, these values should be widely shared among all stakeholders including the administrators, the faculty and staff, students, and the parents. Ideally, this shared value system creates the moral, ethical, and social climate in which EPC behaviors among your staff can flourish. In this kind of environment those who do not make an extensive professional commitment to the school are not the majority of teachers, but in the minority and feel "out of the loop," or out of step with what is valued and expected of them as educators. This will often create enormous positive peer pressure. These shared expectations and attitudes can have very powerful effects on staff members, particularly on the "good" teachers, to commit to a higher and more dedicated level of professional service to the school and to the students they teach.

THE FIVE KEY COMPONENTS TO BUILDING EPC IN YOUR SCHOOL

Through careful team building, modeling, and focused discussions you can create a staff who share core values and hold common beliefs about children, education, academic achievement, and professional excellence within your school. In the Supportive Supervision program your leadership is essential in establishing and promoting the core values, professional behaviors, a child-centered philosophy, and a caring attitude toward children that you expect from each of your staff members.

In the Supportive Supervision program we identify five key elements that sustain an extensive professional commitment: modeling EPC behaviors, asking for a commitment, promoting a child-centered philosophy, encouraging professional dress and demeanor, and providing extra help. While we fully recognize the difficulty of changing teacher behavior, each of these factors plays a role in creating and maintaining a school environment where EPC behaviors can develop and flourish in your staff members.

1. Model EPC Behaviors

Your behavior as a role model for extensive professional commitment is the first and perhaps the most important element in creating an environment to facilitate your teachers' making a similar commitment. Securing an extensive professional commitment from all of your staff will require all your leadership qualities and human relations skills. It hardly needs to be said that as the instructional and administrative leader of the school or department, your actions carry great consequence. In many ways, in the eyes of your staff your character and the actions you take are far more important than your words. Teachers will look to see what you do, not what you say.

As teachers are clearly role models for the students they teach, you, in turn, are a role model for the teachers you supervise. Setting an example by modeling EPC behaviors is the single most effective way you can motivate and effect this change in your staff. For example, as a supervisor you could attend all evening functions and concerts, give extra help to a student, or hold parent conferences at night to accommodate those who work days. Without your functioning as an EPC role model in terms of your own core values and commitment to education, your staff members will see you in a hypocritical position and you will have absolutely no chance to create or develop such values and culture in them.

2. Ask for a Commitment

Using a personal appeal is another way you can motivate your teachers to make an extensive professional commitment. We recommend that you personally invite all members of your staff to make that commitment to your school. As noted above, it is important to clearly express and seek an EPC during the hiring of new staff. Just so, you should seek out and invite existing staff to make a similar type of commitment. No staff member should sit it out on the sidelines; all should be invited to the dance.

In addition to the expectations of teacher performance that were explicitly stated during the hiring process, a personal appeal can be quite an effective tactic for motivating teachers to accept more responsibility and embrace greater levels of professional commitment. For example, asking your language teacher who is a gourmet cook to bring a dish of gnocchi with pesto and help supervise the potluck supper for the parents of new students is a simple matter and might very well work. Similarly, a personal request might just do the trick of encouraging your mathematics teacher, who arrives at 6 a.m. each morning, to supervise an informal, before-school tutoring center.

Sometimes the personal appeal to a teacher to accept additional responsibility will be more complicated. In most school districts the assignment and compensation for extracurricular activities and especially athletic positions are governed by contractual limitations, administrative regulations, board policy, or past practice. For example, it is a common feature in many districts to publicly "advertise" open positions in appropriate places, list minimum requirements for the job, and conduct interviews of all interested parties. Seniority rules often apply, as well. Even here, however, letting someone personally know he or she would be the right person to assume a task or position will often motivate that individual to apply.

3. Promote a Child-Centered Philosophy

Adopting a child-centered philosophy is a third element in creating an environment to secure an extensive professional commitment from every member of your staff. Though this often-quoted concept has almost degenerated into a cliché, placing the needs and interests of children first should be the primary focus of schooling. In the Supportive Supervision program this must become the bedrock philosophy and cornerstone of everything you do in school. In practical terms, the answer to the question, "What is best for the kids?" becomes the determining factor in making all decisions. While we may sometimes disagree on what is best, most often the answer to this question is quite clear. Moreover, there is always value in asking this fundamental question, and we have found that disagreement often helps to clarify issues.

Determining what to do and how to behave based upon what is best for children seems almost too simple a guiding principle, yet the needs and values of kids may often conflict with the needs of others in the school community. For example, teachers might prefer a school procedure that immediately removes a disruptive child, but we may rightly question whether this policy is in the best interests of all children. Similarly, parents may strenuously object to an attendance policy that does not permit students to be "legally" absent from class for a family vacation, yet many would argue that such a strict attendance policy is really in the child's best interest. In this balancing act of conflicting needs, we almost always side with the kids.

The best school environment to support and encourage all staff to make an EPC is one with a child-centered focus. Unfortunately, we have too often observed those who give only lip service to its ideals while they practice contradictions to its moral imperative. Unless a true child-centered philosophy is actively promoted and the decision makers act accordingly, a school will have a very difficult time creating an environment and culture where EPC prevails.

4. Encourage Professional Dress and Demeanor

A fourth factor in creating an environment that supports an EPC culture is professional dress. In the Supportive Supervision program we encourage supervisors not only to act as educational leaders, but to dress the part, too. Moreover, we believe that supervisors should be involved in establishing what is appropriate dress for their staff, as well. School rules about student dress enjoy a lively debate,[57] and indeed styles do vary considerably from school to school, depending upon the climate and socioeconomic and cultural factors. While we will abstain on the contentious issue of uniforms for school children, we do feel that establishing and maintaining a dress standard for the professional staff are important elements in creating an EPC climate. Many research studies have explored the importance of dress and its effect on human behavior.[58] Our own experience confirms what many of these studies show: Dress does matter. Dress is not only a signaling device that elicits certain positive or negative responses in others, but dress greatly influences the wearer, as well. We have found that in school the right kind of professional attire has a positive effect on the demeanor of the wearer, helping to reinforce professional behavior and attitudes. In other words, when we look the part of a caring professional, we behave as such.

Unlike the wide disparity in student dress, what will constitute appropriate professional dress for adults may vary slightly from school to school depending on the region of the country and the location and culture of the school. Of course, the season and climate are factors as well. However, we do feel that it is important that our attire as educators be professional in nature and appropriate for the educational setting and job required. For example, formal business attire would make little sense for a physical education teacher to wear in the gym, just as a jogging outfit or shorts would be out of place in the classroom. We admit to a decidedly conservative bias on matters of apparel for teachers and feel that baggy jeans and Capri pants are best left at home.

Aside from its positive effect on creating an EPC climate, as role models our professional dress and consequent demeanor teach children that schools, similar to houses of worship, are special places where important, life-altering activities occur.

5. Provide Extra Help

A final and critically important element in creating a school climate, which supports extensive professional commitment in staff members, is what has come to be called "extra help." A key strand holding together the diverse threads of the Supportive Supervision program, *extra help* is a generic term used to describe all the informal teaching opportunities that occur between a teacher and student, as opposed to the formal instruction that takes place during regular classroom periods. We encourage you, as a supportive supervisor, to create the opportunities and find the necessary resources for this interaction to occur. The clearest measure of EPC in your teachers will be how often and under what circumstances they extend themselves as professional educators beyond the classroom and reach out to their students to help them achieve.

Five Key Components of EPC

1. Model EPC behaviors
2. Ask for a commitment
3. Promote a child-centered philosophy
4. Encourage professional dress and demeanor
5. Provide extra help

Extra help can occur in small groups or on a one-on-one basis. These teaching opportunities can take place after and/or before school, during lunch periods, or during a teacher's prep, duty, or "free" time. For example, many students and teachers arrive well ahead of the bell to begin the first period of the day. Setting up informal homework and tutoring stations in the library and offices before school begins can accommodate early student arrivals and make it convenient for the "dawn crew" teachers to provide assistance. Regardless of the subject or grade level, all teachers must be encouraged to seek out their students on a one-on-one or small-group basis to help them succeed. This interaction is a vital part of any great school.

A SUCCESSFUL EPC STORY

This following story illustrates how matching the right kind of extracurricular responsibility with the right person can be the principal spark to reenergize and revitalize a teacher's performance in the classroom.

> For several years Mr. Largo taught his eighth-grade English class as if he were on autopilot. Largo was a good teacher, but his lessons were predictable and his classroom performance was uninspiring. Frankly, Mr. Largo's teaching was dull and this was reflected in the mediocre results of his students. His supervisors noted this deficiency on his annual evaluations. Mr. Largo's attempts to improve his classroom performance met with little success.
>
> Now, Mr. Largo's passion was words. Each day after lunch he would routinely knock off *The New York Times* crossword puzzle in less than twenty-five minutes. In ink. In fact, Mr. Largo was an absolute whiz at all manner of word puzzles and games. Recognizing his talent, the principal asked him to design and run a series of afterschool competitions and contests for the middle school academic teams. Reluctant at first to assume this extracurricular responsibility, Mr. Largo soon immersed himself into the task. In time, these spelling, science, social studies, and mathematics contests and games became so popular and so competitive

that they drew large crowds of students who cheered on their classmates. Galvanized by the wild success of this afterschool program, Mr. Largo was stimulated to use similar academic games and methodology in his classes. His renewed enthusiasm for teaching and more engaging lessons resulted in much greater student success than he ever had before. Because of the success he experienced after school doing what he loved, Mr. Largo became a better teacher and expressed a greater professional commitment to his students.

We know of no better example of how assuming a professional responsibility outside of class can make a difference and rouse a teacher to strive for excellence in the classroom.

End-of-Year Evaluation

The sixth and final component in the Supportive Supervisory program is the End-of-Year (EOY) Evaluation. EOY evaluation appears at the top left of the page in the last position in the continuum. EOY evaluation is the final summation that takes into account all of the previous elements, but it also points the way to new goals for the following year. In this chapter we explain how to use a three-part process in producing the EOY evaluation. First, we show how to collaborate with staff to obtain all the necessary evaluative data. We then show how to conduct an annual teacher review conference. Following this discussion, we present the Supportive Supervision EOY evaluation report model. Each of its five sections is described in detail using sample model reports.

Generally, there are two types of teacher evaluation models, summative and formative evaluation.[59] The first makes a judgment on the quality and worth of an individual teacher over a specified period of time, while the latter is less judgmental and focuses on providing enough information to help teachers improve teaching techniques, styles, and strategies. In recent years various schools have experimented with different formative models including portfolio assessment, student and parent surveys, self-evaluation, and peer reviews.[60] Each model has its adherents, yet we support the more traditional summative evaluation model. The purpose of a final evaluation in the Supportive Supervision program is to provide an insightful, comprehensive, and goal-oriented summary of the teacher's professional performance for the entire school year.

Writing annual evaluations is a major administrative responsibility that can take considerable time, analysis, and effort to complete. Usually distributed to staff members at the close of the school year, EOY evaluations often compete for your time with parent meetings, final examinations, annual reports, teacher assignments, special testing schedules, and a myriad of other tasks and items that share roughly the same deadline. As every supervisor knows, there is a madcap finish to every school year.

However, using the Supportive Supervision program and model for writing EOY evaluations can help you lighten this administrative load while providing each teacher with a comprehensive analysis of their pedagogical performance. The raw material that makes up the evaluation (teacher goals and objectives, teacher input, factual data, classroom observations, etc.) has already been created. What remains is a reshaping and repackaging of this material to produce the final product. In our program, EOY evaluation is a collaborative, summative process of analysis, reshaping, and rating. Moreover, because we stress collaboration in the Supportive Supervision program, writing EOY evaluations becomes a shared responsibility and thus more likely to be helpful for the teacher.

EOY EVALUATION IS A PROCESS

> **Supportive Supervision 3-Phase EOY Evaluation Process**
>
> 1. Data Collection
> 2. Teacher Conference
> 3. Written Report

Similar to the method we described earlier for classroom observations, EOY evaluation in the Supportive Supervision program is process driven and has a collaborative focus. For both classroom observation and EOY evaluation, close communication with the teacher and the sharing of information is vital. With open lines of communication and a foundation of trust and mutual respect, the teacher should receive no surprises about what is written or the rating that is assigned. In our program there are three distinct phases to the EOY evaluation process, each of which is an important and necessary step in producing the final document.

Phase 1. Data Collection. In this first stage of the process the supervisor gathers important factual information about the classroom teacher's program, professional responsibilities, classroom performance, and instructional goals and objectives for the current year.

Phase 2. Teacher Conference. In this second stage of the process the supervisor meets with the teacher to discuss and review professional development activities, extracurricular involvement, classroom performance, testing and achievement data, and goals for the following school year.

Phase 3. Writing the Report. Using the EOY evaluation template, all the data parts are assembled, analyzed, and shaped to produce the final written report.

Phase 1. Data Collection

In the Supportive Supervision program the EOY evaluation process begins well before you put pen to paper. Careful planning should take place before any writing is attempted. As is the case with all aspects of the teaching process, good planning will be the key to your success, and more important,

Data Collection
➢ Consult last year's EOY evaluation
➢ Review this year's goals/objectives
➢ Reread observations
➢ Gather achievement and teaching data

to the improvement of your teacher's instructional performance. There are four steps in Phase 1, or the data collection stage: reviewing recommendations in last year's EOY evaluation; analyzing the accomplishment of the individual goals that were established with the teacher at the beginning of this school year; rereading all this year's formal classroom observations; and gathering achievement data and pertinent information related to the teacher's schedule, duty assignments, and extracurricular activities.

Consult Last Year's EOY Evaluation

To begin the EOY evaluation process, it is best to first consult last year's evaluation for all members of your staff. In this document you will find specific recommendations and perhaps goal statements that were established with the teacher at the end of the prior school year. Designed for the teacher to follow in this current school year, these recommendations may be directly tied to classroom performance or related to other professional matters, such as teaching assignments, professional development, or assuming additional school responsibilities. For example, you might have made a recommendation on the EOY evaluation to Ms. Arthur, a veteran science teacher, to pursue professional development opportunities on learning how to incorporate more hands-on learning activities and student demonstration experiments into her teaching.

In this initial step in the process, it will be important to note these recommendations carefully as you review last year's evaluations, for this will serve as a guiding focus and point of inquiry when you meet with the teacher. Did Ms. Arthur attend a methodology workshop and what did she learn? Was it helpful in creating more active student learning and more student-directed lessons? These are the questions that you will want to jot down as you prepare for the meeting with her to review her work for the year.

Goals and Objectives

Reviewing the teacher's individual goals and objectives for this current school year is a second step in the data collection phase of the EOY evaluation process. You will recall that in Chapter 4 we explained the importance of goal setting in the Supportive Supervision program. We recommended that you should not only set personal goals for yourself as a supervisor, but you should collaborate with your staff to establish individual goals and objectives for everyone. Continuing with the Ms. Arthur example, suppose that the instructional goal that had been established with her earlier in the school year was as follows:

To improve student participation and academic performance by planning and incorporating more research experiments, student-led demonstration, and hands-on learning opportunities into her science teaching

This instructional goal then becomes a key focal point for the annual evaluation. Is there evidence that Ms. Arthur incorporated more active learning opportunities? Did academic performance of her students improve? The evidence to answer the first question can easily be found in the lesson plans that were submitted throughout the school year, your direct observations of her teaching, professional development activities she attended, and the discussion you will have at the teacher conference. Evidence for the second question is more elusive. You will have to collect and analyze achievement data to determine if Ms. Arthur's students improved academically. This can be in the form of test results on final exams or course passing rates or achievement levels on standardized achievement tests.

Review Observations

The third item you will want to review will be the classroom observations, particularly focusing on the recommendations that were made. In the Arthur example, suppose that after observing lessons in early October, in December, and then again in April, you had several major recommendations. A few items had to do with improving instructional planning and teaching methodology along the lines discussed previously, while others concerned Ms. Arthur's poor efforts to deal adequately with failing students. You recommended that she follow school procedures on notifying parents of potentially failing students early in the quarter; alter her teaching practices to include more tactile, kinesthetic activities; and to assign and help monitor extra help sessions so students would have an opportunity to turn things around before the end of the marking period.

You will want to note this concern as an item to be discussed with Ms. Arthur in Phase 2 of the EOY evaluation process. Did she contact parents of failing students early in the quarter? Were more hands-on learning opportunities used in her lessons? Were methodology conferences held? Were students assigned to extra help? What were the results? If after the teacher conference you determine that Ms. Arthur has made sufficient progress in addressing this concern, this might be noted as a positive item on the evaluation document. If you determine that substantial improvement did not occur in this area, it should be expressed as a source of serious concern on the EOY evaluation. In other words, a clear and explicit statement to improve parental contact and provide extra help should become twin recommendations on this year's EOY evaluation.

Student Achievement and Teaching Data

A final item in the data collection phase of the EOY evaluation process will be to gather testing and teaching data. By teaching data we mean the specific details about the teacher's program for the year, the number of years in service for the district and school, special assignments and responsibilities, coaching, and extracurricular activities. In Phase 2 of the process, this objective data can be plugged into the EOY evaluation template even before meeting with the teacher. All these data are readily available and should pose no difficulty in assembling.

As has been stressed in No Child Left Behind legislation, gathering and analyzing good testing data offers us an opportunity to focus teachers on their ultimate goal, student achievement.[61] For example, in the case of Ms. Arthur, the best measure of how effective her efforts were in meeting her goals to improve classroom instruction and the academic performance of her students will be student outcomes. Midterm exam results, standardized test results, and the course grades students achieved during the entire school year should all be considered.

Phase 2. Teacher Conference

In our discussion of each of the previous components of the Supportive Supervision program, we have stressed the values of close communication with the instructional staff and collaborative efforts. Collaborating with the teacher is important

> **Teacher Conference**
>
> ➢ Use a teacher input form
> ➢ Discuss this year's goals/objectives
> ➢ Share objective data
> ➢ Agree upon recommendations
> ➢ Rate overall performance

here, as well. In fact, it is a key feature of this second phase of the EOY evaluation process. Here the teacher becomes your partner in the development of the evaluative instrument. Through the use of an input form and an annual review conference the teacher has an opportunity to provide you with valuable data and information that you may not be aware of and that may well become a significant part of the final document. Because of its summative value as an evaluative statement of the teacher's total classroom performance and professional activities for the year, it is important to create a balanced, fully detailed, and accurate picture. At the annual review you and the teacher will want to do several things: review the input form, discuss goals and objectives, share objective data, agree on recommendations for next year, and rate the overall performance.

Teacher Input

One of the best ways to realize a full and balanced teacher portrait is through the use of a teacher input form, which is reproduced in Figure 9.1 in shortened form. We distribute this form a few days before the scheduled meetings and ask teachers to complete it in time for the annual review. The form asks teachers to reflect on their professional activities for the year. On the form, teachers can describe any noteworthy instructional units, professional associations, or any awards or honors that they have received. We also seek information on participation on school committees, attendance at conferences, advisorship of school activities, honors won by students, and so on. In short, we invite teachers to "celebrate" with us this year's success stories.

As often occurs, some teachers will be too modest when describing their professional accomplishments or achievements. It is important to let teachers know that what they accomplish is significant and should be recorded on the final document. Aside from its value as a reflective instrument for teachers, the input form provides yet another way of encouraging teachers to make an extensive professional commitment to the school.

You will notice that all of the information requested on the input form is positive in nature. This is necessary to achieve a complete picture and a balanced report. For example, in referencing the Arthur example described above, suppose on her form she described her afterschool involvement helping the school's music program as a volunteer with the middle school chorus. To give a fair assessment of her professional work for the year, this information should appear on the EOY evaluation, as well as any strongly worded recommendations on improving classroom instruction. While the latter is a far more important matter, the former should not be ignored.

Figure 9.1 End-of-Year Teacher Input

[Form is shortened here.]

EOY Teacher Input

Name _____

Please return by -------> _____

I am in the process of writing your annual evaluations and I need your input. Please be as accurate and as detailed as possible in your response to the following questions. You'll get it back if you are too modest. Now is the time to show me what an excellent job you have done this year.

1. Describe any conferences, seminars, or workshops you may have attended or will attend this year related to last year's EOY evaluation recommendation and/or this year's goals and objectives (in-district or out-of-district).

2. Describe any awards, certificates, recognition, or items of distinction you may have received this year.

3. Describe any awards or certificates received, or competitions any of your students participated in through your assistance and/or encouragement.

4. On what district or school or department committees did you participate this year? (Include staff-development day, in-school observations, and so on.)

(Continued)

Figure 9.1 (Continued)

5. What extracurricular activities did you coach, sponsor, or have a part in this year?

6. What graduate courses, professional development, or inservice credit courses did you take?

7. What professional associations do you belong to?

8. Describe any field trips you have taken or guest speakers you have invited to visit your classes this year.

9. Describe any unit of study, teaching technique, classroom experience, etc. that you feel is worthy of note and reflects positively on your work this year as a teacher.

10. Student Achievement Data: evaluate the testing data that best reflects the academic achievement of your students.

Input From Peers

You may also seek input from peers, especially in writing the EOY evaluation of beginning teachers. As we have noted in our third chapter, on hiring staff, many school districts are establishing formal mentoring programs to help beginning teachers. In most districts mentors are not administrative personnel but experienced classroom teachers with some supervisory training. Mentors can be a primary source of information about the beginning teacher's professional performance and should be involved in the EOY evaluation process. This can be done by meeting with the mentor separately prior to the conference with the teacher.

Conducting the Conference

The importance of conducting an annual review conference with the teacher can hardly be overstated. A review should not devolve into a one-sided discussion. It is best to use the annual review conference as an opportunity for analysis and reflective discussion. In a spirit of collaboration, both the supervisor and the teacher should reflect upon the teacher's professional work for the past year and through a series of questions and data analyses make evaluative judgments based upon it. Ideally, you and the teacher should be able to reach mutual agreement on the contents of the final evaluation document.

Review Goals and Objectives

An important function of the annual teacher conference is to focus the teacher's professional efforts on instructional improvement. The most effective way to do this is to share objective data with the teacher and together assess if the instructional and professional goals that were established at the beginning of the school year were met. Using Ms. Arthur as an example once again, you will recall that her instructional goal for the year was to "improve student participation and academic performance by planning and incorporating more research experiments, student-led demonstrations, and hands-on learning opportunities into her science teaching." You would now discuss with her if she was successful in using more experiments, demonstrations, and hands-on learning activities in her lessons. You will also want to review achievement statistics with her to determine if academic improvement occurred. You will also want to discuss with Ms. Arthur what was learned at the professional development seminar she attended on "Winning Science Strategies" and how she was able to make effective use of what was learned in her planning and classroom teaching.

In the Supportive Supervision program we stress continuity and the cyclical nature of supervisory leadership. A discussion of this year's goal attainment should naturally lead to recommendations for next year. Prepared with objective data and a good understanding of the teacher's professional performance for the year, you and the teacher should try to establish mutually agreed-upon targets and recommendations for the upcoming school year. In the case of Ms. Arthur, since the objective data showed only slight improvement in academic achievement, you might recommend continued efforts to improve instructional delivery and similar professional development activities. These explicit recommendations detailed in the EOY document will form the basis of the more formal individual goal setting that will take place early next school year.

Discuss the Overall Rating

We recommend that you leave the discussion of the rating of the overall professional performance of the teacher to the end of the conference. Although this aspect of the EOY evaluation process may appear somewhat awkward, this need not be so. After all the data are analyzed, the classroom performance reviewed, the goals and objectives evaluated, and recommendations made, it is not difficult to reach consensus on the teacher's overall performance for the year. Before making a judgment, simply ask teachers what rating they would give themselves on our five-point scale. It has been our experience that in almost all cases teachers are keenly aware of their own professional performance and do in fact rate themselves quite accurately.

Phase 3. Writing the EOY Evaluation

> ### Writing the EOY Evaluation
>
> ➤ Introduction and factual data
> ➤ Instructional strengths and recommendations
> ➤ Professional growth and recommendations and
> ➤ Extracurricular activities and recommendations
> ➤ Summary with rating

The third and final phase in the EOY evaluation process is the actual writing of the report. Similar to the observation template, in the Supportive Supervision model we utilize a structured essay format for the written report. In our program the EOY evaluation document contains five parts: an introduction and factual data, instructional strengths and weaknesses, professional growth, extracurricular activities, and a summary with rating. We recommend comprehensive coverage for each of the five parts of the document.

Part One: Introduction and Factual Data

Designed to introduce the teacher to the reader of the document, this opening paragraph should contain accurate information about the district and school where the teacher is employed; the number of years of experience the teacher has in the school; and the subjects, program, courses, and/or grade levels taught. It is best to open or conclude this introductory paragraph with an evaluative sentence giving a general or descriptive statement about the teacher. The following samples of introductory paragraphs of EOY evaluation documents include all basic and relevant information on the teacher in a simple, straightforward format:

Mr. Philip Johnstone has successfully completed his first year at Madison High School. He spent the previous six years teaching science at Palmer Independent Academy in Central City. This year Mr. Johnstone's teaching program consisted of two sections of Sequential III Advanced and two sections of Sequential II, and Sequential II lab classes. Mr. Johnstone has made a satisfactory adjustment from private to public school teaching and demonstrates a capacity and willingness to grow professionally.

Mrs. Kathleen Walpole has completed an outstanding year of teaching in the English Department at Feldman High School. This year, Mrs. Walpole taught one section of English 10, two semester sections of Creative Writing, two semester sections of the senior mandate English 12 RX, and the English 12 Advanced Placement course. Aside from her duties as English teacher, Mrs. Walpole also has teaching responsibilities in the school's Talented and Gifted Program. Mrs. Walpole has completed twenty years of service in the Morris Gable School District, the last eighteen at Feldman.

Ms. Patricia Suarez has completed nine years of professional service in the Glassboro School District. This is her seventh year as a social studies teacher at Thornberry Middle School. Her schedule this year included three sections of eighth grade social studies and two sections of seventh-grade honors social studies. Ms. Suarez is truly an outstanding educator who demonstrates a genuine love of children and a passion for teaching.

Notice that all three samples are relatively short, and that the language used is somewhat formal in tone. Similar to the observation model discussed in Chapter 6, the EOY evaluation is best written in a professional, business-like style. Notice that in the first and third examples, a general evaluative statement comes as the last sentence in the paragraph, whereas in the second sample it comes first.

Part Two: Instructional Strengths and Recommendations

This second section is the heart of the EOY evaluation document. It is here that you provide information about the teacher's classroom performance and interaction with students. Here you would discuss the teacher's instructional goals and present any objective or empirical data to show whether or not those goals were met. References to the formal observations that have occurred during the course of the current school year should be made here as well. This is also the section to describe innovative lessons, effective methodologies, and classroom success stories. For best effect, place recommendations for improved teaching performance in clear statements or goals at the end of this second section of the EOY evaluation report.

Using language that seeks to capture her energy and enthusiasm, the following EOY evaluation sample describes the instructional performance of a master teacher and makes value judgments about her strengths in the classroom.

With boundless energy and a dynamic flair, Mrs. Walpole is a teacher who is committed to the art and science of teaching. Mrs. Walpole is masterful at motivating students to work to the best of their ability. Preparing engaging lessons designed to insure that all students are successful, Mrs. Walpole works tirelessly to inspire them to achieve excellence. Last year's student results on the English 12 AP exam is a direct result of her extraordinary ability as a teacher. All of her students recorded a 3 or higher. As she has in the past, each year Mrs. Walpole is eager to try new methodologies and fresh approaches in her classroom. Mrs. Walpole loves the challenges of incorporating new ideas and ways to reach kids. Her enthusiasm for teaching is infectious. As was noted in her classroom observation this year:

> *Students responded eagerly to your directions and were attentive and on task throughout the entire lesson. Your use of small groups for problem solving, and your rapid pacing, dramatic use of voice, movement around the class, quick changes of focus, and expressive gestures all contribute to a great deal of material covered and a snappy classroom environment where students are engaged in learning.*

Each year, Mrs. Walpole establishes new goals to perfect her talent and skills as an educator. This year Mrs. Walpole set herself the daunting task of incorporating the Internet into her classroom. Toward that end, she has incorporated information found "surfing the net" into her classes and used several online sources as a basis for instructional planning and classroom activities. It should be noted that Mrs. Walpole has taken her classes to the Academic Lab on a regular basis to do research in connection with the literature or writing that was under study in the classroom. It is recommended that Mrs. Walpole work with the chairperson on a professional development program to share her Internet expertise with other members of the department.

Notice that in this example, a direct quotation from one of the classroom observations performed during the year is used to illustrate a key feature of Mrs. Walpole's teaching—her fast paced, engaging, and dynamic teaching style. It should also be pointed out that even though Mrs. Walpole is a master teacher, a single recommendation still appears in this section of the EOY evaluation. In this case, it is a formal written request for her to develop a professional development program to share her expertise with colleagues. A second sample follows:

Mr. Johnstone has a good rapport and genuine concern for his students. He constantly praises his students and takes the time to speak to them individually when he is concerned about their progress. Mr. Johnstone's lessons always provide for guided and independent practice, allowing him to be able to circulate around the room and help his students master the aim of the lesson. Mr. Johnstone has made one wall of his classroom into a "remember board" for his students. He continually writes formulas and important concepts on this blackboard so his students can refer to them during classroom discussions. Mr. Johnstone has made good progress toward meeting his instructional goal this year by accurately assessing the needs of his students through data analysis and reteaching the material to his students. This has resulted in an increased passing rate of 81% on the department midterm exam and a 14% increase in the number of students who scored in the A range. However, results for the final quarter show only a 79% passing rate. Mr. Johnstone's planning goals were only partially met. Though his plans were submitted weekly and were well developed and included all aspects of an effective lesson, he must continue to work on improving the pace of his lessons. Mr. Johnstone must avoid personal digressions and follow the instructional plan. Because of this, not all of the planned instructional activities were accomplished during the lesson. It should be noted that Mr. Johnstone has made progress on several other recommendations that were made as a result of classroom observations. It is recommended that Mr. Johnstone develop handouts that include the aim, "Do Now," development, and guided practice for his students. It is also recommended that Mr. Johnstone continue to work on his motivation and the focusing of his students in the classroom. He must become more of a facilitator in the classroom. Mr. Johnstone needs to define and implement a set of classroom procedures for September that will keep his classes in control and manage student responses to guide his classes through fruitful discussions.

In this sample, reference is made to Johnstone's instructional goals with supporting documentation and statistical data referenced to show that they were achieved (passing rate of 79% on the department midterm exam). Notice that a significant amount of space in this section deals with Mr. Johnstone's instructional weaknesses—failure to develop good handouts, problems with lesson pacing, and difficulty in motivating students and maintaining effective classroom management. Reflecting the seriousness of the classroom management problem, the recommendation to improve is written in strong directive language (use of the words *must, needs to,* etc.) and occupies the concluding three sentences of this section of the EOY evaluation document. A third sample follows:

Ms. Suarez approaches all of her lessons with enthusiasm and continually challenges herself to motivate her students to learn and to become actively engaged in the lesson. She believes that all children can learn if they are given the right kind of instruction that meets their particular learning style. She is always searching for new instructional methodologies that will help bring her students along the path to success. She eagerly searches for supplemental motivational material, such as video clips to bring history alive. She creates five-minute video clips with directed questions to make maximum use of instructional time. Her lessons always have a motivational device to spark student interest in the aim question and searches for activities that mirror those found on state assessment tests. Her 93% passing rate on the state exam last year is evidence of her outstanding qualities as an effective teacher who pushes her students to success. She challenges her students to think critically by having them analyze, judge, and evaluate historical events. In her seventh-grade class she created a project in which students had to create a newspaper on ancient civilization. Her eighth-grade class worked on researching with the Internet on how geography impacted history. They also did a fantastic job on creating a newspaper on the Arab-Israeli conflict by conducting a great deal of research. They role-played various people involved in the conflict by writing letters expressing how they felt about the current situation, researched the role of organizations involved in the conflict, and traced this conflict over time with factual information. She is a warm, nurturing person who encourages her students to push themselves and strive for excellence. She develops each of her lessons around the state assessment curriculum and infuses her lessons with multiple-choice questions, scaffold questions, thematic questions, and document-based questions. Her major academic goal this year was to develop a variety of new techniques on the major essay topics since she will be looping with these students next year. She has been very successful in meeting this objective for she has created folders for each student that will keep various study sheets on major topics that will carry over with them to the next grade. Not only is she teaching them the topics that they will see on the state assessment next year, she is also instilling in them good organizational and study skills. To continue on this path of excellence, we agreed that this use of data analysis to inform instructional practices must be identified for every quiz, test, and exam if we are to meet NCLB requirements and foster higher levels of student achievement.

This third example illustrates how effective a celebratory tone can be in writing an EOY evaluation of an outstanding teacher. The quality of Ms. Suarez's classroom instruction is clearly exemplary, and the evaluation documents her excellent work by describing several outstanding class projects and lessons. The evaluation also makes good use of achievement data. The qualities that are common to all great teachers—enthusiasm, passion for teaching, positive expectations for the success of all students, and a warm personality—are described here as well.

Part Three: Professional Development and Recommendations

This third section on the EOY evaluation template is a separate paragraph where you detail information about the teacher's professional growth and development for the year. Aside from creating a record of the activity, detailing PD information here on the annual review can function as a powerful motivational tool to encourage additional teacher growth and development of skills. Here you would reference any graduate study or college courses that were taken by the teacher this year, and you would also describe any inservice courses, seminars, workshops, and/or conferences attended. In addition to these professional development activities, this section should list the teacher's committee work; participation in district, schoolwide, or departmental activities; and mentoring activities. It is also appropriate to mention the teacher's membership in professional organizations or any outside honors or awards that were achieved related to professional responsibilities or community service. For example, we would record a teacher's citizenship award from the local Chamber of Commerce, but would not list the teacher's winning the Order of Moose low-gross bowling trophy.

Because of the increasing importance of continual professional growth to develop new curriculum and improve teaching skills, do not hesitate to make recommendations for a teacher's professional development in this section of the EOY evaluation document. If a teacher needs specific direction regarding professional development, or needs to demonstrate growth in a particular area, it should be placed in this section. Also use this section of the EOY document to record if a teacher has not participated in PD activities during the year or demonstrated no interest in professional growth.

The following samples of the third section on the EOY evaluation show different levels of professional development interest and engagement:

Ms. Suarez is involved in a variety of professional development activities. She serves as an instructional expert in many ways in our department. She is a master of the global history curriculum and willingly gives of her time to the newer members of the history team. In the beginning of the year she volunteered her time to give a workshop on Effective Study techniques, which received positive feedback from her peers. She mentored a student teacher for both the fall and spring semesters. Last summer she wrote curriculum for an interdisciplinary mapping guide for the seventh-grade teachers. She is encouraged to continue her interest in curriculum by participating as an instructional leader in next year's fall writing workshop. In the midst of her busy schedule she still finds time to continue her classes in instructional leadership at Udall University. She is a member of the Association on Supervision and Curriculum Development, the National Association of Social Studies, and the American Association of University Women.

Notice that in this sample, in keeping with master teachers, Ms. Suarez's professional development activities are extensive. Her contributions to her department and school are emphasized. Mention is also made of her volunteer efforts in conducting a workshop and her mentoring of student teachers. All such professional activities should be placed in this third part of the EOY evaluation document.

The following samples show various kinds of professional development activities that can and should be recorded on the EOY evaluation document.

This year Mrs. Walpole was awarded a Teaching Center mini-grant to publish a TAG Journal. As a published writer, Mrs. Walpole encourages her students to seek publication for their own writing. This year six students won writing contest awards, and ten students' works were accepted for publication. Their poetry, essays, photographs, and stories appeared in High School Writer and Teen Inc. Mrs. Walpole also accepted the important responsibility and did an outstanding job as the Chairperson of the Philosophy and Goals Committee for the Middle States self-evaluation process. It is recommended that Mrs. Walpole continue to assume leadership opportunities at Central High where her writing expertise can make a substantial contribution to the school's success.

Mr. Pagnano has continued to deepen his own commitment to professional growth and development. In the fall, Mr. Pagnano participated in an important series of workshops training ESL teachers on how to prepare students for the new state English assessment and how to grade the completed tests. In the spring Mr. Pagnano also took the District Administrative course, which is designed to encourage selected teachers to apply for supervisory positions and to develop their administrative skills. This summer he will begin a graduate program in Educational Administration and Supervision at State University. Mr. Pagnano also did an outstanding job as the chairperson for the English section of the Middle States Evaluation program. He also presented an excellent workshop for Middlebury faculty and staff during November's Staff Development Day on the electronic grade-book program called "Making the Grade." It is recommended that Mr. Pagnano assume planning committee responsibility for next year's professional initiative program.

Unfortunately there can be times when there may be little or nothing to record. It is important that discussion encouraging a teacher's participation take place throughout the year. When there is a lack of response to the supervisor's discussion, it must be indicated, as we do not recommend skipping this section on the EOY evaluation. Recording that a teacher participated in no professional development activity does serve an important purpose. It underscores the importance of PD as a vital aspect of teaching, and it gives you the perfect opportunity and the strongest possible vehicle to recommend that the teacher pursue professional development. The following example illustrates how such a recommendation can be written in clear and direct language:

Participation in professional development activities is vital for all teachers. Keeping current with the latest methodologies, acquiring new skills, and learning effective teaching techniques are essential for success in the classroom. Mr. Dunne did not attend any conferences or workshops this year. For next year, it is recommended that he attend at least one workshop on using technology to implement the new Marine Biology/Ecology state standards as well as a series of workshops on differentiated instruction. He is also encouraged to join professional organizations such as the National Science Teachers Association where he can take advantage of their resources.

Part Four: Extracurricular Activities and Recommendations

In the Supportive Supervision EOY evaluation template the fourth paragraph describes the teacher's extracurricular activities and service to the school. Devoting an entire section of the document to extracurricular activities highlights the importance that is placed on a teacher providing professional service to the school above and beyond the classroom. This section should reflect the teacher's contributions to the school's total educational program.

As you would expect, teachers who have a strong extensive professional commitment to the school will provide a great deal of information on the teacher input form for you to use in writing the final document. While the wealth of information from EPC teachers may seem to be too much, it is important to include every item mentioned. To do less might give the false impression that you undervalue the teacher's hard work and dedication to the school.

The following EOY evaluation samples describe the extracurricular activities of teachers with EPC:

Mr. Boynton was active in various school activities. He assisted in the organization of and served as a judge for the Barton Lane Science Fair. Seven of his students were among the top ten at the fair and represented Barton Lane at the Regional Science Congress where he also served as a judge. Two of the seven received honors at the Congress. Mr. Boynton also had students participate in the National Science Olympiad Examination in Life Science this year, where the top ten scores were posted by his students. Mr. Boynton also serves as Head Varsity Boys Soccer Coach and Assistant Varsity Boys Lacrosse Coach. Both teams were undefeated; this is the third year Mr. Boynton's teams have achieved this distinction. Mr. Boynton serves as the announcer for all home football games and participated as a field coach on Lacrosse Day. In addition, Mr. Boynton participated in the afterschool You Can Do It extra-help program. Finally, Mr. Boynton organized and led his seventh-grade students on field trips to The Golden Science Center and the Parkward Aviation Museum in Fairview.

Ms. Del Monte has continued her extensive commitment to Harry High School's extracurricular program. Once again, she served as district facilitator for RACE (Russian American Cultural Exchange). In November she coordinated the Russian exchange program, providing outstanding academic, social, and cultural experiences for the visiting Russian students and staff. Ms. Del Monte also is the advisor to Harry's Key Club, which participated in a variety of community and school activities. This year the Key

Club took First Place honors in the State Major Emphasis Program and Second Place State honors in the Read and Lead Program. Ms. Del Monte also finds the time to be the school's study skills facilitator, providing much needed support to the school staff's using study skills methodology. Ms. Del Monte also was accepted as a Delegate Leader and Chaperone for the People to People Student Exchange Program. Finally, this year Ms. Del Monte gave valuable assistance to students as a teacher for the Afterschool Success program and English Assessment Review.

Notice that in both of the preceding samples, the teachers' various activities and service are not merely listed, but celebrated as making valuable contributions to the life of the school. Mr. Boynton's science students achieve distinction and honors at regional fairs under his guidance, while Ms. Del Monte provides "much needed support to the school staff" and "outstanding academic, social, and cultural experiences" for her students. It is important to express the value these awards and honors have for the students and the positive impact on the school's social, cultural, and athletic programs.

Unfortunately, there will be much less to celebrate in this part of the EOY evaluation with teachers who lack an extensive professional commitment. Similar to the point made in Part Three, on professional development, a lack of activity in this area will provide you with an excellent opportunity to encourage and direct the teacher to become involved as the following samples show:

For the past sixteen years Mr. Henry has been advisor to the school's rifle club, which finished the year undefeated and division champs. Three individual team members competed in the Deacon Mills State championship competition and finished in second place. His expert guidance has contributed to the marksmanship of his team. He is commended for his efforts with the team, but as a math educator he is encouraged to become more involved in the afterschool Mathletes program.

Although Mrs. Brooks did not participate in the extracurricular program this year, she has expressed an interest in advising a club next year. She should meet with the Student Activities Director to discuss available advisorships. As a member of the Career/Technical Department, Mrs. Brooks must also take a more active role in the Future Business Leaders of America organization to help her business students apply business concepts learned in the classroom to practical use in regional and state competitions.

In the first sample above, Mr. Henry is commended for his work with the rifle team but is urged to become more involved in an academic activity. In a similar manner, Ms. Brooks is urged to accept additional responsibilities beyond the classroom for the following school year. If teachers do not participate at all in extracurricular activities, recommend that they do so. Because extracurricular activities and sports are so necessary for the social and emotional development of students, as well as the professional growth of teachers, it is important not to omit this section when writing EOY evaluations.

Part Five: Summary Statement and Rating

In many ways the closing paragraph is the most important on the EOY evaluation document because it contains the clearest evaluative language and concluding statement on the teacher's total performance for the school year. Most important, the last paragraph should clearly assign an overall rating for the current year and point to goals and objectives for the following school year.

The rating you assign on the EOY evaluation document should come as no surprise to the teacher. In following our program, the yearly rating will have been discussed and mutually agreed upon at the annual review conference held with the teacher prior to writing the evaluation. Similar to the bottom-line rating of formal observations, use a five-point rating scale for EOY evaluations: unsatisfactory, satisfactory, good, very good, and excellent. Criteria for both rating scales should be provided to the teacher in the beginning of the school year. The specific criteria will vary from district to district and from school to school within a district, but whatever the details are, it is important that they be communicated to the teacher. A teacher rated "very good" will want to know how to become "excellent." Perhaps it will have something to do with the teacher's lack of extracurricular involvement, or mediocre student outcomes, or it may be something else that separates "very good" from "excellent." Such a discussion on ratings can yield very fruitful results and go a long way toward improving a teacher's overall professional performance.

The final statement in the EOY evaluation can also reference individual or departmental goals for the following school year. Most often these goals have not been fully developed by the end of the school year, so rather than an explicit written goal statement, it may be best just to point in that general direction. The summary statement can also be used to explain how the teacher can move to the next level of performance.

The following samples of concluding paragraphs illustrate different levels of professional performance. The first two illustrate how a summary statement may be written in an effusive style for a truly outstanding teacher:

From the beginning of the day to the end of the day, Ms. Suarez is surrounded by children or a faculty member who is trying to get some advice. Thornberry Middle School is lucky to have such a talented and dedicated professional. For all of these reasons she was selected for the highest recognition: Thornberry Middle School Teacher of the Year. It has been another excellent year for Ms. Suarez.

Mrs. Walpole continues to epitomize the very highest standards of professional excellence. As a master English teacher and Talented and Gifted facilitator, she is an invaluable asset to the school. Because she is a totally involved and caring professional and embodies the very best in our profession, Mrs. Walpole is a true role model for all teachers at Feldman High School. For this school year Ms. Walpole's performance is rated as excellent.

Less effusive in style, and much more directive in content, are the summary statements of teachers who are rated as "satisfactory" or "good," as the following samples show:

Mrs. Roundtree has made significant strides toward meeting this year's individual goals, which were to become more organized and to improve her questioning technique with students during lessons. Next year she should continue to create and implement creative lessons, and continue to work on improving classroom management methodology and organizational skills. This has been a good year for Mrs. Roundtree.

This year Mr. Harroldson worked with his chairperson on methods to motivate his at-risk students. Next year he must concentrate his efforts on improving the quality of classroom instruction to help all his students succeed. For this school year Mr. Harroldson's professional performance is rated as satisfactory.

We recommend that tenured teachers who are rated as unsatisfactory for the year be placed on a special intensive supervision program for the following school year.[62] Details of such programs, which are often spelled out in board of education policy, might include a description and list of the educational deficiencies, weekly submission of lesson plans, assignment of a mentor or chairperson to work with the unsatisfactory teacher, peer reviews, inservice mandates, frequent classroom observations, and periodic progress reports. Nontenured teachers who are rated as unsatisfactory should not be retained.

This year Mr. Krahler experienced great difficulty in managing routine classroom procedures and tasks. In addition, his discipline and control of students has greatly deteriorated. Student outcomes were very poor, as measured on the state assessment of basic skills. For this school year Mr. Krahler's professional performance is rated as unsatisfactory. The supervisory provisions of district policy #1665 will be in effect for the following school year.

LOOKING AHEAD

As we have shown here, the EOY evaluation can serve as a starting point for professional growth for the following year. In a way, EOY evaluation is both an ending and a beginning. Produced at the end of the school year, the EOY evaluation is a final document providing a fair and accurate summation of the year's work. It is also a beginning, for it points the way toward goals and objectives for the following school year. In a real sense the EOY evaluation is a bridge connecting one year of professional activity and growth to the next year. If we adhere faithfully to the principles of the Supportive Supervision program, our teachers will see EOY evaluations as truly comprehensive and supportive documents, written confirmations of all their hard work. In the end they will serve your teachers as a vital road map showing where they have been and where they need to go, pointing the way toward continued instructional and professional improvement.

IN SUMMARY

As we have seen in each of these chapters, the Supportive Supervision program is a dynamic, fully integrated, collaborative, and process approach to educational supervision. Recognizing the preeminence of instructional leadership, grounded in a philosophy that places the needs of children first and puts a premium on hiring the "right" teachers, the Supportive Supervision program will provide you with the knowledge and the guidance to develop the skills and behaviors you will need to become a "teacher of teachers." By studying and using the suggested methodologies described in each of the six major components of our program—Goal Setting, Lesson Planning, Observation, Professional Development (PD), Extensive Professional Commitment (EPC), and End-of-Year Evaluation (EOY)—we are confident that you will gain a richer and a deeper understanding of what it means to be a supportive supervisor.

We are certain that as you implement the program, the new knowledge that you acquire and the important administrative skills that you gain will ensure your continued growth and success as a professional educator. With Supportive Supervision as a guide, in time you will not only become an outstanding instructional leader, but you will create a caring teaching staff of true excellence and begin to build a great school that is focused on student success.

The vital importance of what we do as the "teachers of teachers" of children deserves no less of us than our total commitment and dedication to educational excellence. Supportive Supervision validates the importance of that commitment to excellence and embraces the challenges that we face as educators each day as we do our best to prepare our teachers and our children for the future.

Supportive Supervision

INDIVIDUALIZED GOALS
- Classroom management skills
- Lessons containing all essential components
- Lessons responsive to the curriculum

END-OF-YEAR EVALUATION
- Factual data
- Summary of Progress: instructional/ professional development
- Involvement in school activities
- Bottom-line rating

LESSON PLANS
- Review for aim, motivation & summary
- Peer support
- Review organizational activities

The New Teacher

EXTENSIVE PROFESSIONAL COMMITMENT
- Match assignment to interest & ability
- Extra help

OBSERVATION
- Build on strength; minimize weakness
- Be selective
- No more than 3 recommendations
- Be supportive
- Rate the lesson

PROFESSIONAL DEVELOPMENT
- Peer observations
- Faculty workshops, staff-development days, department conferences
- Small-group workshops

Supportive Supervision

INDIVIDUALIZED GOALS
- Recapture enthusiasm
- Match skill & interest to techniques for instructional improvement

END-OF-YEAR EVALUATION
- Factual data
- Summary of Progress: instructional/ professional development
- Involvement in school activities
- Measure & rate year's progress

LESSON PLANS
- Supervisory review of new skills
- Share resources
- Peer support

The Marginal Teacher

OBSERVATION
- Build on strength; minimize weakness
- Look for integration of new skills & make recommendations for improvement

EXTENSIVE PROFESSIONAL COMMITMENT
- Reenergize in activities according to interest

PROFESSIONAL DEVELOPMENT
- Workshops in new skills
- Peer observations
- Teachers teaching other teachers

Endnotes

1. See Jeffrey Glanz and Susan Sullivan, *Supervision That Improves Teaching: Strategies and Techniques* (Thousand Oaks, CA: Corwin Press, 1999) for a discussion of the links between academic achievement and leadership behavior.

2. All statistical data on academic performance of Elmont and New Hyde Park is from *The New York State School District Report Card for Sewanhaka Central High School District: An Overview of Academic Performance* (The University of the State of New York, The State Education Department, 2001).

3. Many of the concepts expressed in this section on goal setting have their roots in the management theory of Peter Drucker, whose ideas on "management by objective" many acknowledge to be the most influential of the 20th century. See Peter F. Drucker, *Management: Tasks Responsibilities Practices* (New York: HarperBusiness, 1993); and Peter F. Drucker, *The Essential Drucker: Selections From the Management Works of Peter F. Drucker* (New York: HarperCollins, 2001).

4. Madeline Hunter, *Mastery Teaching* (Thousand Oaks, CA: Corwin Press, 1995) and *Improved Instruction* (Thousand Oaks, CA: Corwin Press, 1996).

5. C. Glickman, S. Gordan, and J. Ross-Gordon, *SuperVision and Instructional Leadership: A Developmental Approach*, fifth edition (Boston, MA: Allyn & Bacon, 2001). Chap. 10 has an excellent discussion on how and when to use a collaborative model of supervision.

6. C. Glickman, S. Gordan, and J. Ross-Gordon, *SuperVision and Instructional Leadership: A Developmental Approach* (Boston, MA: Allyn & Bacon, 2001); Allan Glatthorn, *Differentiated Supervision*, second edition (Alexandria, VA: Association for Supervision and Curriculum Development, 1997); D. Beach and J. Reinhartz, *Supervisory Leadership: Focus on Instruction* (Boston, MA: Allyn & Bacon, 1999); and Thomas Sergiovanni, *Principalship: A Reflective Practice Prospective*, fourth edition (Boston, MA: Allyn & Bacon, 2001).

7. See Glanz for a discussion of different supervisory models and a good resource of traditional and alternative supervisory structures.

8. Many educational researchers and historians cite the appearance of this report by the National Commission on Excellence in Education as the beginning of the modern school-reform movement. A complete copy of the entire report with all the testimony, findings, and recommendations can be downloaded at http://www.ed.gov/pubs/NatAtRisk.

9. All the information about Effective Schools and its program is taken from the organization's official Web site at http://www.effectiveschools.com/.

10. For a recent critique of the Effective Schools program see Peter Daly, "Recent Critiques of School Effectiveness Research," *School Effectiveness and School Improvement* 11:1 (March 2000): pp. 131-143. See also Roger Slee and others, *School Effectiveness for Whom? Challenges to the School Effectiveness and School Improvement Movements* (London, UK: Routledge Falmer, 1998).

11. Anderson Pellicer, Kelley Keefe, and C. McCleary, "High School Leaders and Their Schools," in Volume 2 of *Profiles of Effectiveness* (Reston, VA: National Association of Secondary School Principals, 1990). This study was the third in a series of national studies of the high school principalship dating back to the early 1960s. Its major purpose was to analyze and describe high school leaders and their schools. This volume describes the characteristics and behaviors of high performing principals ("type A") and typically performing principals ("type B") as they relate to school effectiveness, and it identifies the administrative and programmatic similarities and differences between effective schools administered by principals described as "type A" principals and those administered by "type B" principals.

12. Linda Avila, "Just What Is Instructional Leadership Anyway?" *NASSP Bulletin* 74:525 (April 1990): pp. 52-56.

13. See National Commission on Mathematics and Science Teaching for the 21st Century, *Before It's Too Late: A Report to the Nation From the National Commission on Mathematics and Science Teaching for the 21st Century* (2000) for more information about this critical shortage. Chaired by former astronaut and Senator John Glenn, the report focuses attention on the challenges of math and science teacher recruitment, preparation, retention, and professional growth, and describes specific action steps that can be taken to address these challenges.

14. Statistical projections about the growing teacher shortage come from Recruiting New Teachers Inc., a national nonprofit organization founded in 1986 to improve the nation's teacher recruitment and development policies and practices. They can be found online at http://www.rnt.org.

15. For an interesting look at the personal qualities, interpersonal skills, and values that are exhibited by inspirational teachers, see Robert W. Burke and Iris Nierenberg, "In Search of the Inspirational in Teachers and Teaching," *Journal for a Just and Caring Education* 4:3 (July 1998): pp. 336-354.

16. For a review of various state and local efforts to recruit quality teachers see Michael Allen, *Teacher Recruitment, Preparation and Retention for Hard-to-Staff Schools* (2000; Education Commission of the States, Denver, CO); and Samuel A. Southworth, "Wanted: Two Million Teachers," *Instructor* 109:5 (January-February 2000): pp. 25-27.

17. In New York, as in most states, authority is vested in the local district Superintendent of Schools, while in the Chicago school system teachers and administrators are hired and fired by Local School Councils. See Todd Ziebarth, *The Changing Landscape of Education Governance* (1999; Education Commission of the States, Denver, CO) for a basic understanding of the changes taking place within all areas of education governance.

18. Recruiting New Teachers, Inc., *Learning the Ropes: Urban Teacher Induction Programs and Practices in the United States* (Belmont, MA: Recruiting New Teachers, 1999).

19. Harry K. Wong, "Mentoring Can't Do It All," *Education Week* (August 6, 2001): p. 46.

20. Susan Moore Johnson, "Retaining the Next Generation of Teachers: The Importance of School Based Support," *Harvard Education Letter* (July/August 2001).

21. National Center for Education Statistics (NCES), *Condition of Education* (1997). Available online at http://nces.ed.gov/nces/pubs/ce/c970d01.htlm; and G. Robinson, *New Teacher Induction: A Study of Selected New Teacher Induction Models and Common Practices* (1998; ERIC Document Reproduction Service No. ED424 219).

22. Peter F. Drucker, *Management: Tasks, Responsibilities, Practices* (New York: HarperBusiness, 1993); and Peter F. Drucker, *The Essential Drucker: Selections From the Management Works of Peter F. Drucker* (New York: Harper Collins, 2001).

23. Sam Walton, *Sam Walton. Made in America: My Story* (New York: Bantam Books, 1993).

24. For excellent insights and a discussion of the problems encountered by beginning teachers and their need for supportive professional relationships see Amy De Paul, *Survival Guide for New Teachers* (Washington, DC: U.S. Department of Education, Office of Educational Research and Improvement, 2000).

25. Recent research has shown that marginal teachers have three common behaviors that have negative effects on student learning: failure to create an appropriate classroom atmosphere, lack of personal insight and motivation, and unwillingness to accept responsibility for problems. See Cleaster M. Jackson, "Assisting Marginal Teachers: A Training Model," *Principal* 77:1 (September 1997): pp. 28-29, for a discussion on ways to motivate the marginal teacher to improve performance in the classroom.

26. This lesson is adapted from an AskERIC Lesson Plan #AELP-WCP0054 submitted by Christine Lenoir (July 1999).

27. Robert A. Gamble and Others, "Cooperative Planning for Regular Classroom Instruction of Students With Disabilities," *Preventing School Failure*, 37:4 (1993): pp. 16-20; John F. Riley, "Collaborative Planning and Decision Making in the Elementary School: A Qualitative Study of Contemporary Team Teaching" (2000; Research Report, ERIC Document No. ED447134); and Morton Inger, "Teacher Collaboration in Secondary Schools," *Centerfocus* Number 2 (Berkeley, CA: NCRVE, 1993).

28. The keynote address at the President's Conference on Teacher Quality in September 1999 can be read online at the U.S. Department of Education's Web site at http://www.ed.gov/inits/teachers/conferences/rwraddress.html.

29. Reflective practice can be a beneficial process in teacher professional development, both for preservice and inservice teachers. See Joan M. Ferraro, *Reflective Practice and Professional Development* (2000; ERIC Digest); and especially D. A. Schon, *Educating the Reflective Practitioner: Toward a New Design for Teaching and Learning in the Professions* (San Francisco: Jossey-Bass, 1996). Schon introduced the concept of reflective practice in 1987 as a way for beginners in a discipline to recognize consonance between their own individual practices and those of successful practitioners.

30. See Charles Bruckerhoff and Others, "Celebration of Excellence, 1986-1996," *Summative Evaluation* (The Connecticut State Department of Education, 1996) for a discussion of how one statewide teacher recognition program had a positive impact on restoring teachers' sense of pride in work, self-confidence, and

self-esteem. See also Janice J. Ulrikson, *Perceptions of Secondary School Teachers and Principals Concerning Factors Related to Job Satisfaction and Job Dissatisfaction* (Ph.D. diss., University of Southern California, 1996) for a related study. The findings indicate that teachers viewed the work itself, achievement, responsibility, recognition, and possibility of growth as factors that contributed to their feeling good during a satisfying job experience. They derived the most job satisfaction from recognition, achievement, and the work itself.

31. Thomas S. Dickinson and Thomas Erb, *We Gain More Than We Give: Teaming in Middle Schools* (National Middle School Association: Columbus, OH, 1997); and John W. Alspaugh and Roger D. Harting, "Interdisciplinary Team Teaching Versus Departmentalization in Middle Schools," *Research in Middle Level Education Quarterly* 21:4 (1998): pp. 31-42.

32. This lesson is adapted from an AskERIC Lesson Plan #AELP-APM0201 submitted by Steffanie Broyles and Kiersten England (February 1, 2001) that was adapted from an activity by Cynthia Lanius at http://math.rice.edu/~l anius/pro/rich.html.

33. Richard Ehrgott and Others, "A Study of the Marginal Teacher in California" (Paper presented at the Annual Meeting of the California Educational Research Association, San Francisco, November 1992), ERIC Document No. ED356556. Other researchers suggest that the percentage has a narrower range (5% to 15%). Pamela Tucker, "Helping Struggling Teachers," *Educational Leadership* 58:5 (February 2001): pp. 52-55.

34. Cleaster M. Jackson, "Assisting Marginal Teachers: A Training Model," *Principal* 77:1 (September 1997): pp. 28-29.

35. Richard Ehrgott and Others, "A Study of the Marginal Teacher in California" (Paper presented at the Annual Meeting of the California Educational Research Association, San Francisco, November 1992), ERIC Document No. ED356556.

36. Joan C. Henderson-Sparks and Others, "Managing Your Marginal Teachers," *Principal* 74:4 (March 1995): pp. 32-35; and Kusum Singh and Linda M. Shifflette, "Teachers' Perspectives on Professional Development," Research Report presented at the Annual Meeting of the Eastern Educational Research Association (1993), ERIC Document No. EJ531737.

37. One California researcher presented a research report that looked at the evolution, development, and thinking behind eight different lesson-plan formats. See Keyes B. Kelly, "Evolution/Role of Lesson Plans in Instructional Planning" (Paper presented at the Annual Reading/Literacy Conference, Bakersfield, CA, 1997).

38. Madeline Hunter, *Mastery Teaching* (Thousand Oaks, CA: Corwin Press, 1995), especially chap. 2 on "Decisions in Teaching"; and Madeline Hunter, *Improved Instruction* (Thousand Oaks, CA: Corwin Press, 1996).

39. Keyes B. Kelly, "Evolution/Role of Lesson Plans in Instructional Planning" (Paper presented at the Annual Reading/Literacy Conference, Bakersfield, CA, 1997).

40. Allan Glatthorn, *Differentiated Supervision*, second edition (Alexandria, VA: Association for Supervision and Curriculum Development, 1997).

41. See Patricia Wheeler, *Improving Classroom Observation Skills: Guidelines for Teacher Evaluation* (Livermore, CA: EREAPA Associates, 1992). Wheeler provides practical advice and guidelines on how to prepare for, conduct, and

use classroom observations in evaluating teachers and making personnel decisions.

42. See Jeffrey Glanz and Susan Sullivan, *Supervision That Improves Teaching: Strategies and Techniques* (Thousand Oaks, CA: Corwin Press, 1999) for a discussion of different supervisory models and a good resource of traditional and alternative supervisory structures.

43. The decade of the 1990s saw increased use of collaborative and peer models of classroom observation. For an excellent example and discussion of this approach see Karen H. Peters and Judith K. March, *Collaborative Observation. Putting Classroom Instruction at the Center of School Reform* (Thousand Oaks, CA: Corwin Press, 1999).

44. Annick Brennen, "Clinical Supervision" 2 Oct 2002 <http://www. soencouragement.org/clinical-supervision-case-study.htm>; see also Robert Goldhammer, Robert H. Anderson, and Robert J. Krajewski, *Clinical Supervision: Special Methods for the Supervision of Teachers,* third edition (New York: Holt, Rinehart and Winston, 1993).

45. See Karen H. Peters and Judith K. March, *Collaborative Observation. Putting Classroom Instruction at the Center of School Reform* (Thousand Oaks, CA: Corwin Press, 1999).

46. Wheeler, p. 5.

47. See J. John Loughran, "Effective Reflective Practice: In Search of Meaning in Learning About Teaching," *Journal of Teacher Education* 53:1 (January-February 2002): p. 33(11); S. D. Brookfield, *Becoming a Critically Reflective Teacher* (San Francisco: Jossey-Bass, 1995); and K. E. Osterman and R. B. Kottkamp, *Reflective Practice for Educators: Improving Schooling Through Professional Development* (Thousand Oaks, CA: Corwin Press, 1993).

48. On January 8, 2002, President Bush signed into law the No Child Left Behind Act (NCLB) of 2001. The Act makes substantial reforms in the Elementary and Secondary Education Act (ESEA) that was enacted in 1965. According to the official Web site, NCLB "redefines the federal role in K-12 education and will help close the achievement gap between disadvantaged and minority students and their peers. It is based on four basic principles: stronger accountability for results, increased flexibility and local control, expanded options for parents, and an emphasis on teaching methods that have been proven to work." You can find detailed information on the No Child Left Behind Act of 2001 at <http://www.ed.gov/offices/OESE/esea>.

49. See Steve Cordogan, "A Four-Year Contrast Between High School Students in Interdisciplinary and Discipline-Based Curriculum Programs: Behavioral and Academic Implications" (Paper presented at the Annual Meeting of the American Educational Research Association, Seattle, WA, April 10-14, 2001, Eric Document No. ED461672); Sandra Mathison and Melissa Freeman, "The Logic of Interdisciplinary Studies," Report Series 2.33 (1998), ERIC Document No. ED418434 (1998); and Nancy Flowers, Steven B. Mertens, and Peter Mulhall, "What Makes Interdisciplinary Teams Effective? Research on Middle School Renewal," *Middle School Journal* 31:4 (March 2000): pp. 53-56.

50. See J. John Loughran, "Effective Reflective Practice: In Search of Meaning in Learning About Teaching," *Journal of Teacher Education* 53:1 (January-February 2002): p. 33(11); and Donna L. Ross, "Cooperating Teachers Facilitating Reflective Practice for Student Teachers in a Professional

Development School," *Education* 122:4 (Summer 2002): p. 682(6) for a good overview of reflective practice in education.

51. Belinda Ho, "Using Lesson Plans as a Means of Reflection," *English Language Teaching Journal* 49:1 (January 1995): p. 66.

52. The National Standards Board is a voluntary certification system. Based on what accomplished teachers should know and be able to do, it consists of an innovative two-part assessment process that spans several months: a portfolio of materials to demonstrate how candidates' teaching meets National Board standards and an Assessment Center experience where candidates respond to computer prompts about subject matter and classroom situations, based on the standards developed for their field. See the National Board for Professional Teaching Standards (NBPTS) at http://www.nbpts.org.

53. See New York State Education Department at http://usny.nysed.gov/licensing/teachercertlic.html.

54. A very good synopsis and critique of Lee Canter's Assertive Discipline system can be found at http://www.humboldt.edu/~tha1/canter.html.

55. See Thomas J. Sergiovanni, *Moral leadership: Getting to the Heart of School Improvement* (San Francisco: Jossey-Bass, 1992).

56. Stephen P. Gordon, "The Good School," *Florida Educational Leadership* 1:2 (2001), pp. 13-15, discusses ten attributes of what today's school should have. His list includes compassion, wholeness, connectedness, inclusion, justice, peace, freedom, trust, empowerment, and community. See also Timothy J. Cook, "Soul Searching: What Are Your School's Core Values?" *Momentum* 30:3 (1999), pp. 22-25; and Deborah Grubb, Jeanne Osborne, and Daniel Fasko, "Core Values: After Three Years of Research, What Do We Know?" (Paper presented at the Annual Meeting of the Mid-South Educational Research Association, New Orleans, November 1998).

57. Todd DeMitchell, Richard Fossey, and Casey Cobb, "Dress Codes in the Public Schools: Principals, Policies, and Precepts," *Journal of Law and Education* 29:1 (2000): pp. 31-49.

58. See Joanne B. Eicher, Suzanne Baizerman, and John Michelman, "A Qualitative Study of Suburban High School Students," *Adolescence* 26:103 (Fall 1991): pp. 679(8); "You Are What You Wear," *Financial Management* (CIMA) (December 2000), p. 34, 1p; and Herbert W. Lovelace, "Dressing for Success in a Tough Economy," *InformationWeek* Issue 880 (March 18, 2002); and "Professional Look a Big Plus for Job-Seeking Graduates," *PA Times* 22:10 (October 1999): p. 34.

59. Saany Says, "New Practices in Teacher Education," *School Administrators Association of New York State* 4:5 (1998).

60. See M. Martha Lengeling, *The Complexities of Evaluating Teachers 1996*, ERIC Document No. ED399822; Charlotte Danielson and Thomas L. McGreal, *Teacher Evaluation to Enhance Professional Practice* (Alexandria, VA: Association for Supervision and Curriculum Development, 2000); and Richard P. Manatt "Feedback From 360 Degrees," *School Administrator,* 54:3 (March 1997).

61. NCLB legislation now requires the annual testing of all students in elementary, middle, and high schools. States must establish a single, statewide accountability system that will be effective in ensuring that all districts make adequate yearly progress. You can find detailed information on the No Child Left Behind Act of 2001 at the official NCLB Web site at http://www.ed.gov/offices/OESE/esea.